Table of Contents

Divine Revelation Now

A Theological Exploration

by

Dr. ant

endorses the information the organization or website may provide or recommendations it may make.

Please remember that Internet websites listed in this work may have changed or disappeared between when this work was written and when it is read.

Contents

<u>**Glossary of Key Terms**</u>

<u>**Selected Bibliography**</u>

Introduction

In a world teetering between the scientifically explainable and the ineffable mysteries of existence, divine revelation remains a pivotal element in the theologies of Christianity. This book embarks on a journey to illuminate the modern revelation of God through the astute teachings of theological giants like Augustine, Gregory of Nazianzus, Karl Rahner, Hans Urs von Balthasar, and Blessed Elena Guerra. Each of these thinkers, while rooted in their distinctive historical and cultural milieus, offers us profound insights into the divine articulation that transcends time.

Divine revelation has ever been the heartbeat of Christian theology. As the Scriptures affirm, "For the wisdom of this world is foolishness with God" (1 Cor. 3:19), suggesting that human comprehension reaches its zenith only when it apprehends the divine truths imparted through revelation. Augustine, a luminary of early Christianity, posited that God's truth is not merely an intellectual grasp but a lived experience of divine love. His writings invite us to see God not simply as an abstract principle but as an exquisite, intimate reality manifest in the Trinity.

Conversely, the vantage points of Rahner and von Balthasar enrich our understanding of revelation within a contemporary context. Rahner's "anonymous Christianity" suggests that divine revelation is accessible implicitly, even outside explicit Christian settings—a revolutionary thought that encourages an inclusivity grounded in God's misericordia (mercy). Von Balthasar, with his dramatic theology, unveils a vision of divine truth that is as beautiful as it is redemptive, emphasizing the aesthetic dimensions of God's self-revelation.

Yet, the exploration would be incomplete without considering the eloquent but often overlooked voice of Blessed Elena Guerra. Her insights into Pentecost as the ongoing revelation of the Holy Spirit ignite a renewed fervor in the Christian soul, urging believers to experience the dynamic presence of God in the here and now. Pentecost, as recounted in Acts 2:4, where "they were all filled with the Holy Ghost, and began to speak with other tongues, as the Spirit gave them utterance," stands as a most vivid illustration of continuous revelation.

None of this would be valuable if not for the synthesis of these perspectives which this book endeavors to achieve. Modern times demand an amalgamation of ancient wisdom and contemporary thought, striving for a holistic comprehension of divine revelation. Philosophers and scientists, just as much as theologians, grapple with the intersection of faith and reason—an endeavor Augustine, Gregory, Rahner, von Balthasar, and Guerra were each, in their ways, deeply invested in.

In approaching the divine mystery, one must remember Augustine's assertion that understanding follows faith ("Crede, ut intelligas" - "Believe so that you may understand"). Our inquiry here is not solely an intellectual expedition but a pilgrimage of faith seeking beyond the veils of empirical reality. Gregory of Nazianzus enhances this thought through his intricate Trinitarian theology, showcasing how the relational dynamics within the Trinity offer a model for understanding the interconnectedness of human and divine natures.

"This book summons all who have ears to hear," as it is written, "He that hath ears to hear, let him hear" (Mark 4:9). The calling is for you to engage not just in theoretical reflection but in contemplative immersion. Each chapter delineates the distinct yet convergent paths these thinkers take toward revealing the ultimate transcendence of God. Our goal is not to dilute their theological contributions but to present them as varied facets of a singular, divine truth.

Revelation, in its truest essence, transcends the linearity of time. It is both the ancient whisper in the desert and the stirring call in the modern metropolis. By integrating historical and modern perspectives, we strive to present a comprehensive understanding that speaks to the hearts of the faithful, satisfies the inquiries of the philosophers, and stands up to the rigor of scientific scrutiny. This integrative approach ensures that the discourse on divine revelation remains relevant and profound, unfettered by the confines of any one epoch or academic discipline.

As we delve deeper into the diverse teachings of Augustine, Gregory, Rahner, von Balthasar, and Guerra, it's essential to remember that their voices harmonize rather than compete. Each offers a lens through which the divine mystery becomes a little clearer, a bit more approachable, yet never fully comprehensible, for "Great is the mystery of godliness" (1 Tim. 3:16). The chain of divine revelation is only as strong as its links — the concepts, doctrines, and theologies articulated by our predecessors become our stepping stones to greater spiritual and intellectual enlightenment.

Prepare, then, to tread on hallowed ground. This is not merely a book of theology; it is a sacred dialogue extending through ages, inviting each of us to partake in the unfolding act of divine revelation. As you engage with the thoughts and meditations laid forth in these chapters, may your spirit be awakened to the infinite beauty and truth that transcends human understanding. Let us heed the wisdom imparted through Augustine's intimate reflections, Gregory's intricate theological constructs, Rahner's groundbreaking ideas, von Balthasar's dramatic aesthetics, and Blessed Guerra's fervent devotion.

The revelation of God is an ongoing symphony—notes of ancient wisdom mingling with chords of modern insights. This harmonious interplay beckons us to a fuller, richer encounter with the Divine, one that inspires love, invigorates faith, and kindles the flame of hope within us. As the Psalmist sings, "O taste and see that the Lord is good" (Ps. 34:8), we embark on this journey not only to taste but to feast on the manifold revelations of God, savoring each theological nuance and divine whisper therein.

Let this Introduction be but the first sip from the wellspring of divine wisdom awaiting you in the ensuing chapters.

Chapter 1: The Nature of Divine Revelation

The question of divine revelation has echoed through the halls of human history, compelling saints and scholars alike to ponder how the infinite God communicates with finite beings. Revelation, in its essence, is the unveiling of that which is hidden; it is God making Himself known to humanity. This foundational concept is intertwined with the fabric of Holy Scripture, tradition, and the living experience of the Church.

From the earliest patriarchs who heard the voice of God, to the prophets who cried out in the wilderness, divine revelation has always been a cornerstone of faith. "Long ago at many times and in many ways, God spoke to our fathers by the prophets, but in these last days he has spoken to us by his Son" (Heb. 1:1-2). The pivot from prophetic revelation to the more profound and personal revelation in Jesus Christ marks a significant evolution in our understanding of God's communication with humanity.

Yet, the idea of divine revelation is not stagnant; it expands and adapts to the questions and challenges of each age. While the Scriptures form the bedrock of revelation, the lived experience and theological reflection of the Church help illuminate its depths. The Fathers of the Church, medieval theologians, and contemporary scholars all contribute threads to this rich tapestry. Understanding divine revelation involves stepping into this ongoing conversation, a dialogue as old as the faith and as new as the latest theological inquiry.

Revelation is at once both universal and particular. It speaks to all ages and yet touches each soul uniquely. This duality is intrinsic to its nature. The universal aspect is captured in the Holy Scriptures, inspired texts that convey divine truths applicable to all. The particular aspect, however, is found in personal encounters with God. Consider, for instance, Moses at the burning bush or Paul's dramatic conversion on the road to Damascus. These moments of particular revelation serve as catalysts for personal transformation and communal guidance.

Modern theological thought, propelled by minds like Karl Rahner and Hans Urs von Balthasar, has sought to bridge the timeless truths of scripture and tradition with contemporary existential questions. Their work emphasizes that divine revelation is not merely a historical event but an ongoing process. Rahner's concept of the "anonymous Christian" reveals a broadened understanding of revelation that includes those who may not explicitly know Christ but live in the grace of God. Rahner suggests that God's self-communication extends beyond the confines of explicit faith. "For the grace of God that bringeth salvation hath appeared to all men" (Titus 2:11).

Theologians like von Balthasar push the boundaries further, focusing on the dramatic interplay between divine love and human freedom. Divine revelation, for him, is akin to a divine drama where each soul is called to participate in the unfolding mystery of salvation. In this view, revelation is not static; it dances and interacts with the freedom of the individual, presenting an invitation rather than a coercive decree. "Behold, I stand at the door, and knock: if any man hear my voice, and open the door, I will come in to him, and will sup with him, and he with me" (Rev. 3:20).

Moreover, the interplay of revelation and tradition is a dynamic process. The Second Vatican Council taught that "sacred tradition and sacred Scripture form one sacred deposit of the word of God" (Dei Verbum, 10). This interconnectedness highlights that revelation is both transmitted through and interpreted by the life of the Church. As new generations encounter the divine mysteries, tradition provides a wellspring of wisdom, a living interpretation of revelation that evolves without severing its roots.

Divine revelation also compels us to confront the limitations of human language and comprehension. How can the finite describe the infinite? How can earthly words capture heavenly truths? Yet, God, in his condescension, allows himself to be known through analogies, symbols, and metaphors. "For now we see through a glass, darkly; but then face to face: now I know in part; but then shall I know even as also I am known" (1 Cor. 13:12). This provisional nature of our understanding does not diminish the reality of revelation but invites humility and a deeper yearning for that which is ultimately beyond full human grasp.

The revelatory act of God, as seen in the pages of Scripture and echoed in the lives of saints, prophets, and ordinary believers, invites a response. It is not a one-sided declaration but a divine summons to relationship. This aspect of revelation calls for a transformative engagement, where the recipient of divine revelation is not only enlightened but also called to a profound personal change.

In conclusion, the nature of divine revelation is a symphony of God's self-disclosure played out in human history and individual lives. It bridges the ancient and the modern, the universal and the particular, inviting all to enter into the mystery of God's loving communication with His creation. As we engage with this profound reality, we touch upon the eternal dialogue between the Creator and the created, a conversation that continues to unfold in depth and beauty across times and spaces.

Historical Overview of Revelation

Theological inquiry often embarks on a journey through time, tracing the evolution of divine revelation across epochs. The notion of revelation as the disclosure of divine truths did not emerge in a vacuum; it is deeply rooted in historical contexts, illuminated by sages and Saints. In the Old Testament, revelation began with the patriarchs, such as Abraham, who were granted divine encounters and covenants. God's words to Abraham, "I am the Almighty God; walk before me, and be thou perfect" (Gen. 17:1), encapsulate an early call to a covenantal relationship characterized by obedience and faith.

During the prophetic era, the dynamic of revelation evolved. Prophets like Isaiah and Jeremiah became vessels through which God communicated His will to the people of Israel. These divine disclosures came often as oracles of hope and warnings, thereby shaping the moral and spiritual landscape of the nation. Isaiah's vision in which he exclaims, "I saw also the Lord sitting upon a throne, high and lifted up, and his train filled the temple" (Isa. 6:1), stands as a profound moment of divine glory and holiness imparted to humanity.

Transitioning to the New Testament, the Incarnation of Christ epitomizes the zenith of divine revelation. Through Jesus, God's Word made flesh, the abstract became tangible. In the Gospel according to John, it is written, "And the Word was made flesh, and dwelt among us, full of grace and truth" (John 1:14). This declaration underscores the belief that in Jesus, the divine mystery was fully revealed, a cornerstone for Roman Catholic theology.

The early Church Fathers, including St. Augustine, continued to delve into the depths of divine revelation. Augustine's "Confessions" illustrate a personal and philosophical quest for divine truth. He mused upon the nature of God and emphasized that revelation was integral to understanding the divine essence. His exegesis often reflected on Scripture, such as Psalms, "Thou hast made us for thyself, and our heart is restless until it finds its rest in thee" (Ps. 62:1), underscoring the soul's ultimate yearning for divine communion.

With the advent of medieval scholasticism, theologians like Thomas Aquinas sought to harmonize faith and reason. Aquinas posited that revelations found their fulfillment in divinely infused knowledge, integrating Aristotelian logic with theological truth. By dissecting revelations through such a philosophical lens, Aquinas enriched the theological tapestry, allowing a nuanced understanding that faith and reason are not mutually exclusive but are rather complementary.

The Reformation brought about radical shifts in theological discourse regarding revelation. Martin Luther's assertion of "sola scriptura" emphasized the primacy of Scripture as God's revealed word, accessible to all believers. This paradigm shift underscored the immediate and personal nature of divine revelation, diverging from the perceived intermediaries and hierarchical structures that characterized the Catholic approach. As the Epistle to the Romans declares, "So then faith cometh by hearing, and hearing by the word of God" (Rom. 10:17), Luther's theology returned to this scriptural proclamation, advocating a direct, unmediated reception of divine truths.

In the modern era, theologians like Karl Rahner and Hans Urs von Balthasar have further explored the dimensions of revelation, adapting it to contemporary existential questions and contexts. Rahner's concept of "supernatural existential" postulates that all human beings possess an intrinsic orientation towards God, making the reception of revelation an inherent aspect of human existence. On the other hand, von Balthasar emphasized the aesthetic and dramatic dimensions of revelation, seeing it as unfolding in the dramatic interplay of divine and human freedom.

The Second Vatican Council (1962-1965) signaled a pivotal moment in modern theological exploration of revelation. "Dei Verbum," one of the council's key documents, articulated a nuanced understanding of divine revelation, emphasizing that it unfolds through both Scripture and Tradition. The council reaffirmed that God reveals Himself in history, progressively and intimately, guiding humanity towards the ultimate truth. As stated, "God, who through the Word creates all things and keeps them in existence, gives men an enduring witness to himself in created realities" (Dei Verbum, 3).

In the contemporary theological landscape, there remains a concerted effort to integrate historical theologies with modern insights. Theologians continue to draw from the rich wellspring of Augustinian and Thomistic traditions, merging these with contemporary existential and phenomenological perspectives. This ongoing dialogue reflects a commitment to understanding divine revelation as a living and dynamic reality, continually engaging with the human condition across ages and cultures.

Finally, throughout history, the trajectory of divine revelation is one hallmarked by an ongoing interplay between mystery and manifestation. From the patriarchal revelations to the prophetic visions, from Christ's incarnate mission to the contemplations of mystics and theologians, God's self-disclosure remains an inexhaustible mystery, inviting humanity into deeper communion and reflection. As echoed in Paul's words, "For now we see through a glass, darkly; but then face to face" (1 Cor. 13:12), the journey of understanding divine revelation is both a historical and eschatological pilgrimage, ever beckoning towards the fullness of divine light.

Modern Perspectives on Revelation

The history of divine revelation has been rich, unfolding through the ages as a tapestry woven from the threads of human experience and divine interaction. This perennial stream has not dried up in the modern age; rather, it has evolved and taken on new dimensions through contemporary theological insights. Modern perspectives on revelation seek to bridge the historical understanding with today's existential and intellectual challenges, reflecting an ongoing dialogue between the eternal Word and our temporal context.

Modern theologians like Karl Rahner, Hans Urs von Balthasar, and Elena Guerra have provided fresh viewpoints that balance the traditional with the contemporary. Their contributions underscore the significance of revelation not merely as a static deposit of faith, but as a living, dynamic encounter with the divine. Revelation is thus seen as relational, dialogical, and transformative, always pointing humanity towards a deeper understanding of God's love and plan.

Revelation, in the modern context, is profoundly relational. Karl Rahner, a Jesuit theologian, emphasized the idea of revelation as God's self-communication. In Rahner's view, God reveals Himself not just through words but through an intimate relationship that invites humanity into a participatory experience of divine life. This aligns with Biblical scripture where it is stated, "He that hath my commandments, and keepeth them, he it is that loveth me: and he that loveth me shall be loved of my Father, and I will love him, and will manifest myself to him" (John 14:21).

Hans Urs von Balthasar adds another layer of understanding by focusing on the aesthetic dimension of revelation. He proposes that divine revelation is akin to a dramatic performance where God is the ultimate playwright, and humanity is invited to participate in the unfolding of this sacred drama. According to von Balthasar, the beauty of God's revelation can be seen in the life, death, and resurrection of Jesus Christ, which he views as the culmination of divine self-disclosure.

Von Balthasar's approach also underscores the transcendent and immanent aspects of the divine mystery. He suggests that the cross and the resurrection are not just historical events but are timeless truths that reveal the very heart of God. As the Apostle Paul eloquently puts it, "For the preaching of the cross is to them that perish foolishness; but unto us which are saved it is the power of God" (1 Corinthians 1:18).

Turning towards a more charismatic and pneumatological approach, Elena Guerra advocates for a renewed focus on the Holy Spirit in the life of the Church. She saw the Spirit as the principal agent of revelation in the contemporary world, a view that finds its scriptural basis in Christ's promise, "But the Comforter, which is the Holy Ghost, whom the Father will send in my name, he shall teach you all things, and bring all things to your remembrance, whatsoever I have said unto you" (John 14:26).

Guerra's emphasis on Pentecost underscores the idea of ongoing revelation. She believed that the Church must be continually renewed in the Spirit to stay faithful to its mission. This pneumatological focus resonates with many in the modern charismatic movements, who see the gifts of the Holy Spirit as vital to understanding and living out God's revelation in today's world.

This relational and dynamic nature of revelation is a theme that surfaces repeatedly in modern theology. It challenges traditionalists to move beyond a static understanding and embrace a more engaged and reciprocal mode of divine-human interaction. This is not to undermine sacred tradition but to fulfill its true spirit by contextualizing its timeless truths in the lived experiences of contemporary believers.

Furthermore, modern perspectives on revelation invite a more interdisciplinary approach. They incorporate insights from science, philosophy, and other fields to foster a more holistic understanding of divine revelation. The interface between faith and reason becomes a fertile ground where new dimensions of God's self-disclosure can be discerned, keeping in mind the words of the Apostle Paul, "For now we see through a glass, darkly; but then face to face: now I know in part; but then shall I know even as also I am known" (1 Corinthians 13:12).

This interdisciplinary engagement is particularly relevant in addressing the existential questions and doubts that characterize modern society. Theologians today often find themselves in dialogue with scientists, philosophers, and even skeptics, seeking to present revelation not as an escape from reality but as an invitation to encounter the divine in the complexities of modern life. The recognition that revelation is both a gift and a task, something given and something to be deciphered, enriches this discourse.

Moreover, the notion of contextual theology—tailoring theological reflections to the cultural, social, and existential contexts of different communities—is gaining prominence. Modern theologians acknowledge that revelation must speak to the particularities of each age and culture if it is to be truly transformative. This perspective does not undermine the universality of divine truth but affirms its relevance across diverse contexts. Paul's message to the Athenians, "For in him we live, and move, and have our being" (Acts 17:28) captures this universal yet contextual revelation.

The pressing issues of social justice, environmental sustainability, and human dignity are also significant in the discourse on modern revelation. Theologians argue that God's revelation calls us to act justly and love mercy, a call that echoes the prophetic tradition of the Old Testament: "He hath shewed thee, O man, what is good; and what doth the Lord require of thee, but to do justly, and to love mercy, and to walk humbly with thy God?" (Micah 6:8).

In summary, modern perspectives on divine revelation emphasize its relational, dynamic, and transformative nature. The contributions of theologians such as Rahner, von Balthasar, and Guerra reflect a profound engagement with the mystery of God's self-communication in ways that speak to the heart of contemporary concerns. These modern insights do not replace traditional understandings but rather enrich and expand them, providing fresh lenses through which the eternal Word can be encountered anew in the ever-changing landscape of human existence. Such an approach ensures that the divine revelation remains a living reality, continually calling individuals and communities to a deeper understanding and more authentic living out of the divine truth.

Chapter 2: Karl Rahner's Theology of Revelation

Karl Rahner, a seminal figure of 20th-century Roman Catholic theology, offers an intriguing and comprehensive perspective on the revelation of God. Rahner's theology of revelation stands distinct yet integrated within the broader Christian tradition, synthesizing ancient wisdom with contemporary understanding. His approach, deeply rooted in both philosophical inquiry and biblical tradition, seeks to answer how God communicates with humanity in the modern age—a vital inquiry for theologians, philosophers, and scientists alike.

One of the fundamental concepts in Rahner's thought is the idea of the "supernatural existential." This term encapsulates the inherent openness of human nature to the divine, a predisposition that he believes is an existential aspect of our being. Rahner asserts that God has endowed humanity with an innate capacity to recognize and respond to divine self-disclosure. This supernatural existential forms the foundation for understanding how revelation unfolds within human history and individual experience.

For Rahner, revelation is not merely a series of doctrinal propositions handed down from on high. Instead, it is an ongoing, dynamic process that engages the whole person—mind, heart, and spirit. This dynamic nature of revelation aligns with St. Paul's declaration that "now we see through a glass, darkly" (1 Cor. 13:12). Rahner's theology contends that revelation is both historical and personal, a living encounter that transforms those who receive it.

An essential aspect of Rahner's theology is the emphasis on God's self-communication. He maintains that God's ultimate act of revelation is the self-giving in Jesus Christ, "the Word made flesh" (John 1:14). Through Christ, the invisible God becomes visible, making divine mystery accessible and relatable. However, Rahner also believes that God's self-communication extends beyond the historical Jesus, continuing through the Holy Spirit's work within the Church and the world.

Rahner's view on God's revelation in the modern world reflects his understanding of the transcendental nature of human existence. He proposes that God's self-disclosure is not limited to sacred texts or ecclesiastical teaching but permeates all of creation and human experience. This universal scope of revelation is reminiscent of the psalmist's affirmation that "the heavens declare the glory of God; and the firmament sheweth his handywork" (Ps. 19:1).

In Rahner's context, revelation must engage with contemporary culture and scientific advancements. He contends that the modern world, with all its complexities and advances, is not a barrier to revelation but rather a locus where divine self-communication can be understood anew. Thus, theology must dialogue with science, social sciences, and culture to fully grasp the depth and breadth of God's revelation today.

One cannot overlook Rahner's concept of the "anonymous Christian." This idea posits that God's grace operates beyond the visible boundaries of the Church, reaching those who may not explicitly profess the Christian faith yet live in accordance with God's will. According to Rahner, such individuals are implicitly aligned with the truth revealed in Christ, thereby participating in the divine mystery. This inclusive vision echoes the universality of God's salvific will, as expressed in the Pauline letters: "God our Saviour, who will have all men to be saved, and to come unto the knowledge of the truth" (1 Tim. 2:3-4).

Rahner's theology challenges the Church to recognize revelation's multifaceted nature and its accessibility to all people. By affirming the possibility of encountering God's self-revelation in various contexts, Rahner expands the horizons of theological inquiry and pastoral practice. This expansive approach necessitates a Church that is open, dialogical, and responsive to the signs of the times, embodying the incarnational reality of Christ's presence in the world.

Moreover, Rahner's thought underscores the importance of personal experience in the process of revelation. He contends that the existential questions and profound experiences of individuals often serve as the locus for divine encounter. In this perspective, prayer, reflection, and human relationships become crucial mediums through which God reveals Himself. The multiplicity of ways in which God can communicate highlights the personal and relational dimensions of revelation, ensuring that it is not confined to intellectual assent but encompasses the whole of human life.

Rahner's theology also emphasizes the eschatological dimension of revelation. He perceives history as a journey towards the ultimate fulfillment of God's self-communication, a process that finds its culmination in the eschaton. This forward-looking perspective provides hope and meaning, encouraging believers to perceive their lives and the world as part of God's redemptive plan. It resonates with the prophetic vision found in Revelation: "Behold, I make all things new" (Rev. 21:5).

In conclusion, Karl Rahner's theology of revelation offers a profound and expansive understanding of how God communicates with humanity. Grounded in the Christian tradition yet responsive to contemporary challenges, Rahner's insights invite a deeper engagement with the mystery of God's self-disclosure. His emphasis on the supernatural existential, the dynamic nature of revelation, and the universality of God's grace provides a robust framework for understanding revelation in the modern world. In Rahner's vision, revelation is an ongoing, transformative encounter that calls believers to discern God's presence in the complexities of human life and the unfolding history. This vision, rooted in the biblical witness and ecclesial tradition, continues to inspire and challenge those who seek to apprehend the divine mystery in a world that is ever-evolving yet always touched by the transcendent.

Fundamental Concepts in Rahner's Thought

The essence of Karl Rahner's theology of revelation delves into the very heart of the human encounter with the divine mystery. Rahner's approach is characterized by a profound, encompassing vision that seeks to bridge the transcendent and the immanent, the divine and the human. For Rahner, revelation is not merely an isolated historical event but an ongoing, dynamic process sown into the very fabric of human existence.

At the core of Rahner's thought is the concept of the "supernatural existential." This term represents God's grace and self-communication embedded within the human condition from the outset. In Rahner's perspective, every human being is inherently oriented toward God, a notion that aligns with Augustine's famous reflection: "Thou hast made us for Thyself, O Lord, and our heart is restless until it finds its rest in Thee." Rahner builds upon this by suggesting that God's self-gift is the fundamental horizon within which all human experiences and history unfold.

Rahner's understanding of revelation further emphasizes the transcendental experience. He posits that human beings, in their innate openness to the infinite, encounter God's mystery as the ultimate ground of all being. "Be still, and know that I am God" (Ps. 46:10), Rahner might suggest, speaks to the intrinsic capability and necessity for humans to experience God beyond explicit deeds or defined events. This transcendental encounter positions human existence itself as the locus of divine revelation.

This transcendence is complemented by Rahner's insistence on the historical and particular nature of revelation—the "categorical." While the supernatural existential provides the overarching context, revelation also occurs in concrete historical acts, most supremely in the person of Jesus Christ. Rahner sees the incarnation as the definitive manifestation of God's self-revelation, a concept that echoes the prologue of John's Gospel: "And the Word was made flesh, and dwelt among us" (John 1:14).

Integration of the transcendental and categorical elements forms a crucial cornerstone in Rahner's theology. He argues that these two dimensions are not in opposition but rather inextricably connected, mutually illuminating. The historical moments of revelation, the covenants with Israel, and the life, death, and resurrection of Jesus, as described in the Scripture, anchor the continual, existential experience of God's grace. "For now we see through a glass, darkly; but then face to face" (1 Cor. 13:12), this intertwining signifies the complex and layered nature of revelation.

Another significant concept in Rahner's thought is the notion of the "anonymous Christian." In light of his broader vision, Rahner asserts that God's offer of salvation and self-communication extends to all humanity and is not confined to explicit Christian faith. This paradigm-shifting idea recognizes the universal reach of God's grace while affirming the uniqueness and necessity of explicit revelation in Christ. Thus, even those who have not encountered the Gospel in its formal proclamation are, in a sense, already touched by God's revelatory grace, an insight that emphasizes God's omnipresence and omnibenevolent nature.

Rahner's vision also entails a profound eschatological dimension. He perceives revelation as oriented toward the future fulfillment of God's kingdom, wherein the full realization of God's self-gift will unfold. The eschaton, or the ultimate future, is not merely a distant reality but continually interweaving with the present, urging humanity into a deeper participation in divine life. "For our conversation is in heaven; from whence also we look for the Saviour, the Lord Jesus Christ" (Phil. 3:20), echoes Rahner's forward-looking theological orientation.

Rahner's theological framework isn't just about intellectual or doctrinal formulations. It speaks deeply to the lived experience of faith, integrating the mundane aspects of life with the profound mysteries of the divine. This synthesis is a hallmark of

Rahner's thought, harmonizing theology and spirituality. His view of revelation thus becomes a deeply personal and communal journey, where the divine continually beckons, transforms, and fulfills the human spirit's deepest longings.

This comprehensive, unified view of revelation reclaims a sense of awe and wonder in the face of the divine mystery. In today's fragmented world, where the sacred can often seem divorced from everyday life, Rahner's thought reaffirms the inherent sacramentality of all creation. He reminds us that the world is imbued with God's presence, that "the heavens declare the glory of God; and the firmament sheweth his handywork" (Ps. 19:1), making every moment an opportunity for encountering God.

Moreover, Rahner's synthesis provides a robust framework for dialogue with contemporary culture and thought. His openness to the supernatural existential aligns with the aspirations of modern science and philosophy. By acknowledging the divine mystery within the context of human knowledge and experience, Rahner paves the way for fruitful discourse between faith and reason. This approach is crucial for engaging with an increasingly secular world while preserving the depth and integrity of theological tradition.

In summary, Karl Rahner's fundamental concepts of supernatural existential, transcendental experience, categorical history, the anonymous Christian, and eschatological orientation provide a rich and multifaceted approach to the theology of revelation. They call us to recognize the pervasive and transformative presence of God's self-revelation in both the sublime and the ordinary, in human striving and divine grace, in historical events and existential realities. Rahner's vision invites theologians, philosophers, scientists, and believers alike to a deeper contemplation of the divine mystery unfolding within and beyond time.

Rahner's View on God's Revelation in the Modern World

Karl Rahner, throughout his extensive theological works, articulated a dynamic vision of God's revelation in the modern world. His approach is both deeply rooted in traditional theology and strikingly attuned to contemporary existential realities. Rahner's vision revolves around the concept that divine revelation is not a static or historical phenomenon, but a perpetual and dynamic event. According to Rahner, God's self-communication must be perceived as a reality that continuously unfolds within the fabric of human history and personal experience.

At the heart of Rahner's theology lies the notion of the "anonymous Christian." This term encapsulates Rahner's belief that God's grace permeates the human experience universally, even when it goes unrecognized. Rahner posits that every person, by virtue of being human, has an innate capacity for God. This capacity translates into a latent potential for revelation, making the divine accessible to all, regardless of their explicit religious commitments. In this regard, Rahner echoes the universality of God's offer of salvation as underscored in the Scriptures: "For there is no respect of persons with God" (Rom. 2:11).

Rahner argued that the modern world, with its advancements in science and technology, its cultural diversities, and its existential quests, is not alien to divine revelation. Rather, these elements can become loci where God's self-disclosure can be encountered. Rahner believed that God's transcendence and immanence are not in opposition but work together to reveal the divine mystery within the ordinary experiences of life. This convergence aligns with the biblical affirmation that "In him we live, and move, and have our being" (Acts 17:28).

A crucial aspect of Rahner's view is the sacramental presence of God in the world, which challenges the dichotomy between the sacred and the secular. He proposed that all reality is, in some sense, sacramental because it has the potential to convey God's grace. Rahner's sacramental understanding invites modern Christians to perceive every-day occurrences, relationships, and even the material world as vessels of divine revelation. This perspective resonates with the holistic vision of creation depicted in Genesis, where God continually affirms the goodness of creation (Gen. 1:31).

Furthermore, Rahner emphasized the importance of existential experience in the process of revelation. He held that God communicates with individuals not through abstract propositions but through their lived experiences. For Rahner, personal history becomes the arena where one encounters God.

This experiential dimension of revelation insists upon an authentic and reflective engagement with one's own life circumstances. It echoes the inner spiritual journey that is vividly portrayed in the Psalms: "Search me, O God, and know my heart: try me, and know my thoughts" (Ps. 139:23).

In reinforcing his views on modern revelation, Rahner did not shy away from the complexities and ambiguities that often accompany human existence. He acknowledged the presence of suffering, doubt, and ambiguity as integral to the human condition. Rather than seeing these elements as obstacles to revelation, Rahner considered them as moments that can lead to a deeper understanding of the paradoxical nature of divine love and mystery. This perspective is illuminatingly portrayed in the paradoxical statement of Jesus: "For whosoever will save his life shall lose it; but whosoever shall lose his life for my sake and the gospel's, the same shall save it" (Mark 8:35).

Rahner's approach also includes a profound respect for other religious traditions, recognizing them as places where God's revelation can also occur. He argued that the Holy Spirit is at work in all cultures and religions, drawing them towards the fullness of truth revealed in Jesus Christ. This inclusive vision is consonant with the Trinitarian belief in the universal activity of the Spirit, as Jesus indicated: "The wind bloweth where it listeth, and thou hearest the sound thereof, but canst not tell whence it cometh, and whither it goeth: so is every one that is born of the Spirit" (John 3:8).

Moreover, Rahner's theology emphasizes the eschatological dimension of revelation, suggesting that God's self-disclosure is both already present and yet to be fully realized. This eschatological tension upholds a hope that transcends the present and invites believers into a future where God's revelation will reach its consummation. Paul's words echo this future orientation: "For now we see through a glass, darkly; but then face to face: now I know in part; but then shall I know even as also I am known" (1 Cor. 13:12).

In education and formation, Rahner's insights prompt theologians and educators to engage with the world critically and creatively. Understanding that God's revelation unfolds in dialogue with the contemporary context, Rahner encourages a theology that listens to the signs of the times while remaining faithful to the core truths of the Christian faith. His stance advocates for a pastoral approach that remains open to the ongoing dynamics of God's self-communication, aligning with the calling to "quench not the Spirit. Despise not prophesyings" (1 Thess. 5:19-20).

Rahner's view insists that revelation is an invitation to an ever-deepening relationship with God, an active participation in the divine mystery. This understanding calls for a faith that is intellectually robust, spiritually profound, and existentially engaged. It is a faith that echoes the wisdom of Ecclesiastes: "He hath made every thing beautiful in his time: also he hath set the world in their heart, so that no man can find out the work that God maketh from the beginning to the end" (Eccles. 3:11).

In sum, Rahner's theology presents God's revelation as an ongoing, dynamic encounter that transcends time and permeates the entirety of human existence. His perspective encourages a posture of openness, reflection, and engagement with the world, fostering a faith that seeks to discern the divine mystery in the manifold realities of modern life. Rahner's legacy invites us to embrace the presence of God in the here and now, ever mindful of the promise and hope of divine fulfillment yet to come.

Chapter 3: Hans Urs von Balthasar's Approach

Hans Urs von Balthasar approached theology with a blend of intellectual rigor and spiritual fervor, seeking to uncover the mysteries of divine revelation in a manner that invites one to behold its profundity. His work is noted for its unique synthesis of the aesthetic, the dramatic, and the theological.

Von Balthasar's starting point is the comprehensive beauty of God. According to him, revelation is inherently tied to the manifestation of divine glory—a glory that can be both seen and experienced. For von Balthasar, this glory is captured supremely in Christ, the Incarnation, where the eternal Word becomes flesh (John 1:14).

The Incarnation is not merely an isolated event in history but is central to understanding all of God's interactions with humanity. In the face of Christ, we see the face of true beauty—a beauty that compels and attracts. As he posits, the whole of God's revelation is encapsulated in the person of Jesus Christ who personifies divine beauty and truth.

This perspective brings a fresh dimension to understanding revelation. Unlike traditional views that often emphasize doctrine and morality, von Balthasar accented the role of aesthetic experience in encountering God. Within his theological framework, the experience of beauty—whether in art, nature, or liturgy—becomes a window into divine revelation.

It is significant to note that von Balthasar did not see beauty as trivial or peripheral. Instead, he argued that the beautiful reveals the very essence of divine truth. "O worship the Lord in the beauty of holiness" (Ps. 29:2) encapsulates this sentiment, asserting that the aesthetic and the sacred are deeply intertwined.

Balthasar's emphasis on beauty is coupled with his profound understanding of the dramatic narrative of revelation, particularly through his work on the concept of "theo-drama." In this framework, he employs the metaphor of a divine play, with God as the playwright who enters into the drama of human history. Jesus Christ is both the central actor and the stage upon which this divine action unfolds. It points to a God who does not remain distant but engages intimately in the human story.

Through this dramatic lens, revelation is not static. It is dynamic, relational, and participatory. The believers are invited into this drama, called to respond to the divine initiatives in their own lives. This response enhances our understanding of revelation as not merely information but as a transformative encounter with the divine.

Moreover, von Balthasar places a strong emphasis on the role of the Church in this divine drama. The Church is not just a passive recipient but an active participant in the continuing revelation of God. The ecclesial community embodies Christ and carries forward the mission of revealing God's beauty and truth to the world. In his words, the Church mirrors the light of Christ, "For where two or three are gathered together in my name, there am I in the midst of them" (Matt. 18:20).

In Balthasar's vision, then, the Church becomes a living testimony to divine revelation, a community of believers continuously engaged in the mystery of God's unfolding story. This makes revelation a communal experience, embedded deeply within the liturgical and sacramental life of the Church.

He also holds a unique perspective on the relationship between nature and grace, one which is integral to grasping his approach to revelation. According to von Balthasar, the natural world itself bears witness to divine glory. By contemplating creation, one is led to contemplate the Creator. This is reminiscent of the Pauline assertion, "For the invisible things of him from the creation of the world are clearly seen, being understood by the things that are made" (Rom. 1:20).

His theology, thus, calls for a unified vision that sees the sacred permeating all aspects of life. This holistic view does not partition the sacred from the secular. Instead, it recognizes the potential for encountering God's revelation in every facet of existence, from the grandeur of the cosmos to the intimacy of human relationships.

Von Balthasar's theology also presents a distinctive eschatological dimension. The final revelation of God's glory will be fully realized in the eschaton, the ultimate consummation of all things. It is here that the beauty and drama of divine revelation will find their complete expression. This eschatological hope is a call to live in the present with eyes fixed on the divine promise of the future, where God "shall wipe away all tears from their eyes" (Rev. 21:4).

This futuristic orientation does not detract from the present moment; rather, it infuses the now with profound significance. We are pilgrims on the way, participants in a divine narrative that moves toward a glorious culmination. This teleological vision provides a context within which current experiences of revelation are appreciated and understood.

In summary, von Balthasar's approach deeply enriches our understanding of modern revelation through its aesthetic, dramatic, and eschatological lenses. His insistence on the centrality of beauty, the narrative character of revelation, and the active participation of the Church offers a dynamic and engaging account of how God continues to reveal Himself to humanity. It beckons us to encounter divine revelation not merely as a set of propositions but as a breathtaking panorama of divine love and glory, drawing us ever deeper into the mystery of God's infinite beauty.

As we journey through the theological landscape shaped by figures like Augustine, Rahner, and von Balthasar, we find our understanding of God's revelation continuously deepened and expanded. The following chapter will offer a comparative analysis of Rahner and von Balthasar's contributions, further illuminating the rich tapestry of modern theological thought.

Core Ideas in von Balthasar's Theology

Hans Urs von Balthasar's theology offers a rich tapestry of thought, interweaving beauty, truth, and goodness with a profound exploration of divine revelation. Central to von Balthasar's theological framework is the concept of aesthetics, or the study of beauty, which he posits as a vital entry point to understanding God's revelation to humanity. For von Balthasar, beauty is not a superficial or supplementary aspect of theology but is intrinsic to all divine self-communication. It serves as the "first word" of God and as an essential dimension of the divine truth.

Von Balthasar contends that the revelation of God cannot be fully comprehended without recognizing the beauty that pervades creation and, more specifically, the life of Christ. The beauty of Christ's sacrificial love on the Cross is a compelling revelation of divine glory. As Scripture declares, "And I, if I be lifted up from the earth, will draw all men unto me" (John 12:32). This attraction, this drawing power, stems from the beauty and sacrificial depth of God's love revealed in Christ.

Another cornerstone of von Balthasar's theological vision is the idea of "theo-drama." This concept frames the interplay between God and humanity as a dramatic narrative where each person has a role to play within God's salvific plan. Unlike static and abstract theological constructs, theo-drama considers the dynamic and relational aspects of revelation. God's interaction with humanity unfolds in a manner akin to a cosmic play, with Christ as the central actor whose life, death, and resurrection are the climactic acts. The Apostle Paul marvelously captures this dynamic in his epistle: "For in him we live, and move, and have our being" (Acts 17:28).

Within the theo-dramatic framework, von Balthasar emphasizes the importance of human freedom and God's call to partnership in the divine drama. This divine-human cooperation does not undermine God's sovereignty but accentuates the dialogical nature of revelation. Humanity is invited to respond freely to God's self-disclosure, participating actively in the unfolding divine plan.

Von Balthasar also addresses the notion of the "analogy of being" (analogia entis), a critical concept for understanding divine revelation. This analogy suggests that there is a real, albeit analogical, correspondence between creation and Creator. However, von Balthasar warns against reducing God to human concepts or experiences. Instead, he sees the analogy as a means to contemplate the infinite through the finite, the eternal through the temporal. This approach fosters a reverence and awe that aligns with the biblical proclamation, "O the depth of the riches both of the wisdom and knowledge of God! how unsearchable are his judgments, and his ways past finding out!" (Rom. 11:33).

Furthermore, von Balthasar's exploration of the Trinity forms a cohesive core of his theology. He posits that the revelation of the Triune God is the pinnacle of divine self-communication. The reciprocity and communion within the Trinity serve as the ultimate model for human relationality and community. The self-giving love between the Father, Son, and Holy Spirit reveals the essence of divine love, providing a template for understanding God's engagement with humanity. "God is love; and he that dwelleth in love dwelleth in God, and God in him" (1 John 4:16).

Von Balthasar also brings to the fore the incarnational aspect of revelation. For him, the Incarnation is God's definitive self-disclosure, embodying both divine mystery and human participation. Christ's life and ministry, culminating in his death and resurrection, are the ultimate manifestations of God's immanent and transcendent nature. Through the Incarnation, God becomes accessible, approachable, and knowable, fulfilling the prophetic vision, "And the Word was made flesh, and dwelt among us" (John 1:14).

In addition, von Balthasar's devotion to Marian theology cannot be overlooked. He views Mary as the paradigm of total receptivity to God's will, embodying the ideal human response to divine revelation. Mary's fiat—"Behold the handmaid of the Lord; be it unto me according to thy word" (Luke 1:38)—captures the essence of faithful submission and openness to God's transformative work in the world. In her, von Balthasar finds a theological exemplar who reflects the Church's role in receiving and transmitting divine revelation.

Moreover, the ecclesial dimension in von Balthasar's theology highlights the role of the Church as the living context within which God's revelation is both encountered and interpreted. He argues that the Church, as the Body of Christ, participates in the unfolding drama of salvation history. The Church is the mediator of divine truth, safeguarding the sacred deposit of faith and facilitating the experience of God's presence through the sacraments. The unity and mission of the Church are grounded in the Trinitarian communion, mirroring the divine relations within the Godhead.

Von Balthasar also places significant emphasis on the eschatological orientation of revelation. He views revelation as not only unveiling the reality of God in the present but also pointing towards the ultimate fulfillment of God's promises. This future-oriented aspect of revelation imparts hope and an active anticipation of the Parousia—the second coming of Christ. Scripture underscores this forward-looking hope: "Looking for that blessed hope, and the glorious appearing of the great God and our Saviour Jesus Christ" (Titus 2:13).

Equally important in von Balthasar's thought is the understanding of suffering within the context of revelation. He views human suffering through the lens of Christ's Passion, seeing it as a participation in the mystery of redemptive suffering. In this regard, suffering becomes a locale of divine revelation where God's solidarity with humanity is vividly manifested. The Apostle Peter captures this truth: "For even hereunto were ye called: because Christ also suffered for us, leaving us an example, that ye should follow his steps" (1 Pet. 2:21).

Lastly, von Balthasar's theological vision is marked by a deep sense of mystery and reverence for the unfathomable depths of God's being. Rather than attempting to demystify the divine, he invites theologians and believers alike to embrace the mystery with humility and wonder. This approach resonates with the biblical admonition: "But as it is written, Eye hath not seen, nor ear heard, neither have entered into the heart of man, the things which God hath prepared for them that love him" (1 Cor. 2:9).

In summation, the core ideas in von Balthasar's theology—aesthetic beauty, theo-drama, the analogy of being, Trinitarian communion, the Incarnation, Marian receptivity, ecclesial participation, eschatological hope, the redemptive nature of suffering, and the embrace of divine mystery—collectively frame his unique approach to divine revelation. Each of these elements interlocks to form a comprehensive and dynamic

Balthasar's Understanding of Revelation Today

Hans Urs von Balthasar's approach to revelation today can be seen as an attempt to reconcile the eternally divine with the temporal human experience. In our contemporary era, Balthasar's understanding becomes vital as it does not merely rest on historical revelation but continually engages with the living and dynamic God. Revelation, for him, is not static but a continual dialogue, a symphony between Creator and creature that unfolds in manifold ways.

Central to Balthasar's conception is the notion of revelation as a dramatic encounter. He envisages revelation in the framework of a divine theater, where God is the ultimate dramatist and humanity the audience and actors. This theater of revelation calls for an active, responsive participation from humanity, where individuals are invited to step into their roles within God's story. This dramatic structure allows for a deeply incarnational experience—a direct engagement with Christ, the Word made flesh, who is the ultimate revelation of the Father.

In Balthasar's view, revelation is not constrained to the words of the Bible alone but is a grand narrative that plays out through the life of Christ. "In the beginning was the Word, and the Word was with God, and the Word was God" (John 1:1). Through the life, death, and resurrection of Christ, the divine narrative reaches its zenith. Every act of Jesus, every parable, and every miracle is a revelation of the Father's love and purpose for humanity. The gospel accounts are not mere historical records but living testimonies that continue to speak God's word anew to every generation.

Yet, Balthasar emphasizes that this divine drama is incomplete without human reception and response. The Word becomes alive when it is heard, accepted, and lived out in the life of believers. "Faith cometh by hearing, and hearing by the word of God" (Rom. 10:17). That hearing is not passive but an active, transformative process where the Word takes root within the believer, germinating into a life lived in consonance with God's will.

Balthasar also incorporates the beauty of God's revelation. For him, beauty is not just an aesthetic experience but a theological necessity. God's beauty, revealed in Christ, acts as a compelling force drawing humanity to the divine. Herein lies the intersection of divine revelation and human freedom—God's beauty is freely given, and humans are free to respond. The encounter with divine beauty, thus, becomes a cornerstone of Balthasar's understanding of revelation today.

In our era of skepticism and relativism, Balthasar's emphasis on beauty as a mode of divine revelation offers a unique pathway.

Beauty transcends mere logical arguments and appeals to the heart. "He hath made every thing beautiful in his time" (Eccles. 3:11). When the divine beauty is seen in the life of Christ or the sacraments, it becomes a pervasive testimony of God's continuous revelation, a silent but poignant invitation to all.

Moreover, Balthasar's appreciation for the ecclesial dimension of revelation cannot be overstated. For him, the Church is not a mere institution but the body of Christ, a continuous font of revelation. The sacraments, the liturgy, and the communal life of the Church are spaces where the divine drama unfolds anew. Revelation is not an individual enterprise but a communal journey where the Church, guided by the Holy Spirit, plays a pivotal role. "For where two or three are gathered together in my name, there am I in the midst of them" (Matt. 18:20).

This communal aspect extends to Balthasar's understanding of tradition and scripture. He sees them not in opposition but in harmonious interplay. Tradition is the living transmission of revelation, ever unfolding through the guidance of the Holy Spirit. Similarly, scripture is not a closed book but a living word that speaks to each contemporary situation. The Church, with its magisterial authority, serves as the authentic interpreter of this dynamic interplay, discerning the word of God in the signs of the times.

In sum, Balthasar's understanding of revelation today is holistic, encompassing the dramatic, beautiful, and ecclesial dimensions. It calls for a receptive and responsive engagement with God's continued self-disclosure. The essence of his approach lies in viewing revelation as a living, dynamic process—a divine-human dialogue that transcends time and culture. Through the lens of this understanding, believers are invited to see the world as a stage where God's grand narrative unfolds, beckoning them to partake actively in the unfolding mystery of salvation.

Furthermore, Balthasar's insights remind us of the sacramental nature of revelation. He emphasizes that every encounter with the sacred, every liturgical celebration, and every sacrament is a fresh manifestation of God's revelation. The Eucharist, the source and summit of Christian life, is the preeminent symbol of God's continual self-giving. "This is my body, which is given for you: this do in remembrance of me" (Luke 22:19). Through the Eucharist, believers are mystically united with Christ, experiencing a profound revelation of divine love.

This perspective challenges the reductionist views of revelation that limit it to mere intellectual assent or historical knowledge. Balthasar invites us to a holistic transformation, where mind, heart, and spirit are engaged in a continuous encounter with God. It's not enough to know about God; one must experience Him. This experiential knowledge is at the heart of Balthasar's revelation—an invitation to dwell in the divine presence and be transformed by it.

As we navigate the complexities of the modern world, Balthasar's approach offers a path rich in depth and meaning. It calls for a reintegration of faith and reason, beauty and truth, individual and community. It beckons us to see revelation not as a distant event relegated to the past but as a present reality, continually inviting us into deeper communion with God.

In the final analysis, Balthasar's understanding of revelation is a call to live fully immersed in the divine drama, to perceive the beauty of God in all things, and to engage actively in the life of the Church. This is a vibrant, living revelation that speaks powerfully to our times, urging us toward a profound encounter with the divine in every moment of our lives.

Chapter 4: Comparative Analysis of Rahner and von Balthasar

The theological landscapes of Karl Rahner and Hans Urs von Balthasar bear distinct contours, yet their underlying terrains share a common heritage rooted deeply in the richness of the Catholic tradition. Both theologians sought to elucidate the mystery of divine revelation, engaging with it not as an abstract notion but as a lived, dynamic experience that permeates human history and consciousness.

Their approaches, however, diverge in methodology and emphasis. Rahner's transcendental theology, profoundly influenced by his engagement with existential philosophy and Thomistic metaphysics, posits that God's self-revelation occurs through the very structure of human subjectivity. Rahner asserts that human beings have an innate openness to the divine, a "supernatural existential" grace that predisposes them to receive God's revelation. In Rahner's words, God's revelation is "always already" present in the depth of human experience, climaxing in the Christ-event.

Balthasar, in contrast, emphasizes the dramatic and aesthetic dimensions of revelation. He approaches theology through the lens of divine beauty and the narrative unfolding of salvation history. For Balthasar, revelation is akin to a divine drama, a

Theo-drama where God's self-disclosure is made manifest in the historical and visible actions of Christ. Unlike Rahner's inward transcendental focus, Balthasar's theology is more extroverted, stressing the incarnational and sacramental presence of God that reaches out to humanity through visible signs and symbols.

What binds Rahner and Balthasar together is their Christocentric focus - their theological enterprise revolves around the person of Jesus Christ as the ultimate revelation of God. Yet, while Rahner might emphasize the epistemological and existential aspects of understanding Christ, Balthasar would draw us to the aesthetic and narrative engagements with Christ's life, death, and resurrection. Rahner sees Christ as the fulfillment of the human quest for meaning, the one who clarifies and completes the transcendental horizon of human existence. In contrast, Balthasar invites us to behold Christ as the central character in the divine drama, whose every act is an event of salvific beauty.

Consider Rahner's belief that revelation is not limited to explicit doctrinal formulations but extends to implicit, everyday experiences shaped by God's grace. Throughout his works, Rahner acknowledges the mystery of God's silence, where revelation can dwell in what remains unsaid, urging believers to engage in a profound contemplation of the ineffable. This is evocative of the biblical sentiment, "Be still, and know that I am God" (Ps. 46:10).

On the other hand, Balthasar is known for his critique of reductionist interpretations that might strip Christianity of its mystery and awe. He insists that theology cannot be reduced to sheer academic exercise; it must involve a profound engagement with the incarnational mystery. Drawing from the biblical imagery, Balthasar's theology reflects the Pauline sense of wonder: "For now we see through a glass, darkly; but then face to face" (1 Cor. 13:12).

In examining the implications of their theological visions for modern theology, one finds that Rahner's thought encourages an engagement with contemporary issues through a theological anthropology that bridges faith and reason. His concept of the "anonymous Christian" envisages a universal potential for salvation, a notion that resonates well with interfaith dialogue and modern inclusivity. For Rahner, the seeds of revelation are sown in the soil of human existence, accessible to all, regardless of explicit religious affiliation.

Balthasar presses modern theology back to its roots in the dramatic encounter with divine revelation. His insistence on the beauty and drama of revelation confronts the modern inclination to secularize or intellectualize faith, calling instead for a return to the tangible, sacramental, and narrative dimensions of Christianity. Balthasar's theology of revelation stands as a bulwark against any attempts to domesticate the gospel, reminding the faithful that revelation is an awe-inspiring, transformative encounter with the living God.

Both theologians challenge modern thinkers to reconsider the parameters of revelation. Rahner requires us to look within, to understand the divine inexorably linked with human being and consciousness. Balthasar forces a gaze outward, to behold the glory and beauty of God made manifest in the tangible world and the narrative of salvation history. These perspectives are not mutually exclusive but rather complementary, each providing a vital lens through which to apprehend the fullness of divine revelation.

The comparative analysis of Rahner and Balthasar underscores the richness of the theological tradition and its capacity to address a myriad of contemporary concerns. Rahner's transcendental method and Balthasar's aesthetic Theo-dramatic approach offer robust frameworks for engaging with the mystery of God in the modern world. Their differing yet convergent paths serve as a testament to the depth and diversity within Catholic theology, encouraging believers to seek a deeper, more holistic understanding of divine revelation.

As theologians continue to explore these frameworks, the landscape of modern Catholic theology will inevitably be enriched by the insights of both Rahner and Balthasar. Their contributions illuminate the multifaceted nature of revelation, inviting the faithful to a more profound encounter with the divine mystery that permeates all aspects of life—both the immanent and the transcendent.

In conclusion, the comparative study of Rahner and Balthasar serves not just as an academic exercise but as a journey into the heart of Christian faith, revealing the manifold ways God chooses to disclose Himself. As we ponder their insights, we are reminded of the divine wisdom encapsulated in the words of Solomon: "It is the glory of God to conceal a thing: but the honor of kings is to search out a matter" (Prov. 25:2). Thus, the pursuit of understanding revelation becomes a sacred task, a quest that urges us to delve deeper into the inexhaustible mystery of God.

Key Differences and Similarities

Delving into the theological tapestries woven by Karl Rahner and Hans Urs von Balthasar unveils a fascinating contrast and convergence. These two giant minds of 20th-century Catholic theology provide distinct yet sometimes harmonizing perspectives on the nature of divine revelation. The speech of Rahner is steeped in existential questions, attuned to the subtleties of human experience and transcendence. Von Balthasar, on the other hand, paints with the broad, dramatic strokes of aesthetic theology, where beauty, love, and divine theater take center stage.

A primary divergence between Rahner and von Balthasar lies in their understanding of the locus of revelation. For Rahner, revelation finds its home within the depths of human subjectivity. He often emphasized the "supernatural existential," a condition imprinted into the very fabric of our being, enabling a constant openness to God's self-communication. In this view, every human encounters the divine implicitly through their transcendental experience, perpetually oriented toward God.

Von Balthasar, contrastingly, focuses on revelation as a divine drama played out in history, with Christ as the ultimate scriptwriter and actor. Revelation is not merely a personal communication; it is an event, a spectacle of divine love and beauty echoing through the narrative of salvation history. His theological aesthetics explore this revelatory drama, viewing creation as a stage upon which God's glory manifests, culminating in the incarnate Word, Jesus Christ.

Both theologians align in recognizing Jesus Christ as the focal point of revelation. For Rahner, Christ represents the concrete expression of the transcendental revelation inherent in human nature. He is the "absolute savior," whose life and message bring to light the implicit presence of God in human history and consciousness. "For in him dwelleth all the fulness of the Godhead bodily" (Col. 2:9), Rahner would affirm, seeing Christ as both the epitome and fulfillment of human existential longing for the divine.

Von Balthasar, in his Christocentric vision, also places Christ at the heart of revelation but in a manner emphasizing the beauty and grandeur of God's self-giving. Christ's existence is a testament to divine glory, a symphonic display of love that beckons humanity to participate in this divine mystery. This portrayal of Christ is not just as a mediator of revelation but as the very epitome of God's aesthetic and dramatic entrance into human history.

Despite these different emphases, Rahner and von Balthasar converge in their sacramental view of the world, albeit through different lenses. Rahner's idea of the "sacramental principle" suggests that everyday realities can mediate God's presence, fostering an encounter with the divine through ordinary experiences and symbols. This principle extends the potential for divine revelation to all of creation, echoing the sacramental theology found in the broader Catholic tradition.

Similarly, von Balthasar views the entire cosmos as a grand sacrament, a visible sign of an invisible grace reflecting the glory of the Creator. His theological aesthetics encourage seeing God's presence in the beauty and complexity of the world, culminating in the ultimate sacrament of Christ. Here, both theologians echo the sentiment that the created order serves as a conduit for divine revelation, though they articulate it through different theological frameworks.

In recognizing similarities, one must note their shared dedication to bridging the gap between divine mystery and human experience. Despite the disparities in their thought processes and emphasis, they both aim to make the profound truths of faith accessible and resonant for contemporary believers. This pastoral dimension ensures that their theological insights remain grounded in the lived experience of faith, rather than abstracted philosophical musings.

Rahner and von Balthasar also share a commitment to the universality of salvation and revelation. Rahner's theology underscores God's grace as universally at work within every individual, emphasizing the inclusive nature of divine revelation. He often spoke of "anonymous Christians," those who, while not explicitly professing faith in Christ, nonetheless participate in this universal salvific grace by virtue of their openness to the transcendent.

Von Balthasar similarly upholds the universal scope of God's redemptive love but emphasizes the dramatic interplay of individual freedom and divine initiative. His theology of hope does not shy away from the profound mystery of human cooperation with grace, trusting in "the Lamb of God, which taketh away the sin of the world" (John 1:29). Here, von Balthasar's focus on the pivotal role of human response to divine love complements Rahner's more existential approach to the same reality.

Moreover, both theologians grapple with the challenge of articulating revelation in a pluralistic world. Rahner's engagement with modern philosophical thought and von Balthasar's dialogue with contemporary culture illustrate their efforts to make the Gospel intelligible in diverse contexts. Their works reflect a robust engagement with modernity while remaining rooted in the timeless truths of the Christian faith.

In conclusion, the comparative analysis of Rahner and von Balthasar reveals a rich tapestry of theological insights where differences enrich and similarities fortify their collective contribution to understanding divine revelation. Whether through the existential depth of Rahner or the aesthetic drama of von Balthasar, both theologians illuminate the multifaceted ways in which God's self-disclosure continues to unfold in human history and experience. Thus, their thought invites a deeper contemplation of the mystery of the divine and calls for a more profound encounter with the God who both transcends and permeates our world. Their collective insights echo the psalmist's declaration: "The heavens declare the glory of God; and the firmament sheweth his handywork" (Ps. 19:1).

Implications for Modern Theology

In the interplay between Karl Rahner's and Hans Urs von Balthasar's different yet complementary perspectives on divine revelation, we find fertile ground for modern theological reflection. Rahner's transcendental approach, which suggests that all humans have an inherent capability to experience God, and von Balthasar's focus on the dramatic revelation of God's beauty and truth in Christ, compel us to rethink how we understand and articulate God's self-disclosure in today's world.

First, Rahner's concept that God is indirectly experienced through the depths of human consciousness challenges us to reconsider the boundaries of divine immanence. This theological position implies that divine mysteries are not only accessible for the devoutly religious but are embedded within the very fabric of human existence. As Rahner proposes, humanity's existential experiences become avenues through which divine truths are revealed. "For now we see through a glass, darkly; but then face to face" (1 Cor. 13:12) serves as a scriptural affirmation of this understanding. The implications here are profound: modern theology must grapple with the idea that God's presence permeates ordinary human experiences, potentially democratizing the experience of the sacred.

Conversely, von Balthasar's emphasis on the dramatic and aesthetic aspects of revelation puts forth a vision where God's truth is unveiled through the life, death, and resurrection of Christ. Von Balthasar views these events not merely as historical facts but as divine acts imbued with aesthetic and dramatic significance. His theology posits that the transcendent beauty and goodness revealed in Christ compel a response and thereby draw humanity into the divine mystery. This perspective presses contemporary theology to embrace a more holistic and existential encounter with God's revelation, recognizing that it speaks as much to the heart as it does to the mind.

Perhaps the most transformative implication of comparing these theological frameworks is the resultant call for an integrated approach to revelation that acknowledges both the transcendental and the dramatic. While Rahner invites us to find God in the transcendental depths of human existence, von Balthasar urges us to recognize the divine narrative enacted through Christ. Thus, modern theology is tasked with creating a synthesis where intellectual and emotional, universal and particular, mystical and historical dimensions of divine revelation are held in fruitful tension.

In an age marked by rapid scientific advancements and growing secularism, such a synthesis becomes crucial for communicating the pertinence of faith. When Rahner's transcendental insights meet von Balthasar's dramatic narratives, theologians are better equipped to dialogue with contemporary culture. This dialogue can bridge the gap between scientific rationality and religious experience, showing that they are not mutually exclusive but instead complementary paths to understanding the divine.

Moreover, such a synthesis has significant implications for ecclesiology and the role of the Church in the modern world. Rahner's theology suggests that the Church must be open to the workings of God's spirit in ways that transcend traditional church boundaries. This calls for an inclusive ecclesial vision that embraces the broader human quest for meaning. On the other hand, von Balthasar's focus on the dramatic unfolding of God's plan in Christ signifies the Church's role as a living witness to this divine drama, engaging the world not just through doctrine, but through compelling narratives and acts of witness.

From an ethical standpoint, the convergence of Rahner's and von Balthasar's thoughts underscores the importance of a lived theology that engages the complexities of modern life. Understanding revelation as both a transcendental and dramatic encounter compels believers to address social injustices, engage in compassionate service, and promote human dignity, all while rooted in a deep, mystical connection to God. "Defend the poor and fatherless: do justice to the afflicted and needy" (Ps. 82:3) becomes an ethical mandate grounded in this dual vision of revelation.

The implications for spiritual formation are equally profound. If God's revelation is both deeply personal and universally significant, then spiritual practices must cultivate both internal transformation and outward engagement. Spiritual formation rooted in Rahner's transcendental theology would emphasize contemplative practices that foster an awareness of God's presence in everyday life. Conversely, inspired by von Balthasar's dramatic theology, spiritual practices would also involve communal worship and acts of solidarity that reflect the narrative of God's salvific work in the world.

Ultimately, the comparative analysis of Rahner and von Balthasar propels modern theology towards a comprehensive understanding of divine revelation. It challenges theologians to develop frameworks that are intellectually rigorous, spiritually enriching, and practically relevant. In so doing, it ensures that the divine revelation continues to shine forth in a world that is ever in search of meaning, truth, and beauty. "For thou wilt light my candle: the Lord my God will enlighten my darkness" (Ps. 18:28).

Finally, this theological synthesis invites laypeople and scholars alike to embrace a faith that is both deeply personal and publicly engaged. It encourages us to seek God in the everyday, while also participating in the grand story of redemption. As we navigate the complexities of modern life, we are called to be witnesses to the transcendental and dramatic revelations of God, embodying a faith that is alive, dynamic, and responsive to the divine call.

Chapter 5: St. Augustine on the Trinity and Revelation

In contemplating the complexity of St. Augustine's theology, one finds a profound intersection of faith and intellect, particularly in his explication of the Trinity and divine revelation. Augustine's thoughts regarding the Trinity, when married with his insights into revelation, offer us an intricate tapestry that continues to resonate within contemporary theological discourse. To understand Augustine's influence on modern revelation, it is crucial to delve into his Trinitarian theology first.

St. Augustine's conception of the Trinity is deeply rooted in his philosophical background and his exegetical reading of the Scriptures. In "De Trinitate" (On the Trinity), Augustine meticulously examines the nature of God as one essence in three persons: Father, Son, and Holy Spirit. This Trinitarian formula is not merely a theological abstraction but a manifestation of divine love and unity. Augustine describes the Trinity as an eternal relationship of love, with the Holy Spirit as the bond that unites Father and Son. This is epitomized by "God is love" (1 John 4:8), suggesting that within the Godhead exists a perfect and eternal communion of love.

Augustine's exploration of the Trinity is not just a speculative venture but serves as a foundation for his understanding of divine revelation. For Augustine, the act of revelation is inherently Trinitarian. The Father reveals Himself through the Son in the power and illumination of the Holy Spirit. This Trinitarian dynamic ensures that revelation is a holistic and immersive encounter with the divine. In a sense, it enacts the unity and distinction within the Godhead, as seen in passages such as "In the beginning was the Word, and the Word was with God, and the Word was God" (John 1:1).

One of the key contributions of Augustine's thought is the idea that divine revelation is both historical and personal. He contends that God's self-disclosure is not confined to a single moment in history but is ongoing, vibrant, and accessible to each believer. This view challenges a static understanding of revelation, positioning it instead as a dynamic interaction between the divine and human realms. His reflections in "Confessions" underscore this, where he narrates his own transformative experience as an enduring revelation, a ceaseless invocation of God's presence in his life.

Furthermore, Augustine's emphasis on the interiority of revelation plays a pivotal role in his theological framework. He posits that God's truth is imprinted upon the human heart, an idea encapsulated in his famous prayer, "You have made us for yourself, O Lord, and our hearts are restless until they rest in you." This intrinsic orientation towards God, this "restlessness," leads to an ever-deepening understanding of divine truths.

Augustine sees this as the movement of the Holy Spirit within, inspiring and enlightening the human mind.

In contemporary theological discussions, Augustine's Trinitarian perspective offers rich insights into the nature of revelation. His notion that revelation is an act of divine love, realized through the relational dynamics of the Trinity, can inform modern interpretations. Especially in an age where the relational aspect of theology is gaining emphasis, Augustine's insights remind us that the content of revelation is deeply tied to the experience of communal love and unity. The Trinitarian model exemplifies how community and revelation are intertwined, helping believers to understand themselves as part of the divine communion.

Moreover, Augustine's insistence on the continual and personal nature of revelation resonates with present-day understandings of experiential and existential theology. His view that God's revelation adapts to the human condition, speaking in various ways across different contexts, anticipates modern theological approaches that emphasize the situatedness and contextuality of divine action. In essence, Augustine prepares us to see God's hand in the ebb and flow of everyday life, transforming ordinary moments into glimpses of the divine mystery.

Augustine also offers a nuanced understanding of Scripture as a primary vehicle of revelation. He believes that the Scriptures are divinely inspired texts that reveal God's plan, but requires the illumination of the Holy Spirit for their true meaning to be discerned. "The letter killeth, but the spirit giveth life" (2 Cor. 3:6). For Augustine, the Bible is not merely a historical document but a living word, eternally effective and personally transformative. His allegorical method of interpretation allows for deep, layered readings that uncover the spiritual dimensions concealed within the literal text.

Considering Augustine's hermeneutic approach, it becomes apparent that understanding the revelation requires both faith and reason. He does not see faith and reason as contradictory but as complementary tools in discerning divine truths. The famous dictum "credo ut intelligam" (I believe that I may understand) signifies this harmony, positing belief as the foundation upon which intellectual exploration is built. In this light, Augustine's theology encourages a deeper engagement with both the spiritual and rational aspects of revelation.

The implications of Augustine's Trinitarian and revelatory theology extend to the realm of ecclesial life. His thought underscores the Church's role as the community where revelation is lived, experienced, and transmitted. In this communal context, revelation is not an individualistic encounter but is mediated through the sacraments, liturgy, and communal prayer. Augustine's vision of the Church as the "body of Christ" (1 Cor. 12:27) intertwined with his Trinitarian theology, underscores the notion that God's revelation unfolds within a communal framework. The Church, guided by the Holy Spirit, becomes the milieu where divine truths are continuously revealed and celebrated.

Moreover, Augustine's theological vision invites modern theologians and believers alike to embrace a holistic view of revelation, one that considers the interconnectedness of the Trinitarian communion, personal experience, and ecclesial life. By doing so, it allows for a theology that is both deeply traditional and profoundly relevant to contemporary concerns. His emphasis on the historical and personal dimensions of revelation aligns seamlessly with current endeavors to integrate historical-critical scholarship with personal religious experience.

In summation, Augustine's contributions to Trinitarian theology and divine revelation provide a rich framework that continues to inform and inspire. His insights encourage us to see revelation not as a static deposit of truths but as a dynamic, Trinitarian act of divine love. This ongoing interplay between the divine and human realms, mediated by the Trinitarian communion, offers a profound and enduring lens through which to view the mysteries of faith. As contemporary theologians, philosophers, scientists, and believers, we find in Augustine a guide who leads us to deeper reflections on the nature of God and the perpetual unfolding of divine revelation.

Augustine's Trinitarian Theology

St. Augustine's contributions to Trinitarian theology are among his most profound and influential works in Christian doctrine. Central to his understanding is the concept of 'God as three in one'—Father, Son, and Holy Spirit—coequal and coeternal. He initiated these ideas not randomly but through extensive scriptural exegesis, philosophical rigor, and a deep, personal faith journey. Augustine's understanding of the Trinity serves not only as an intellectual endeavor but also as a pastoral guide, meant to draw believers into a more intimate relationship with God.

In his groundbreaking work, "De Trinitate" ("On the Trinity"), Augustine articulates a vision where the triune nature of God is reflected in creation and the human soul. He asserts that God can only be known through revelation, as human rationality alone is inadequate to comprehend the divine mystery. Augustine employs the biblical text, particularly the Gospel of John, to substantiate his claims. For instance, he quotes Jesus stating, "I and my Father are one" (John 10:30) to support the unity and co-essential nature of the Godhead.

Augustine emphasizes that the Father, the Son, and the Holy Spirit, while distinct in personhood, are inseparably united in essence. This unity and distinction are not contradictory but are necessary to fully apprehend the nature of God. Augustine likens this divine relationship to human analogies, though he admits their limitations. One such analogy is that of the mind: memory, understanding, and will are distinct yet operationally united aspects of a single human soul. Similarly, the Trinity comprises three distinct persons who are one in nature.

One of Augustine's key contributions is his exploration of the 'psychological analogy' for understanding the Trinity. In this, he suggests that just as the human mind consists of memory, understanding, and will, so too can the triune nature of God be comprehended through the relations of Father, Son, and Holy Spirit. This threefold unity illustrates how unity can exist within diversity, a concept that augments our grasp of divine immanence and transcendence.

In "De Trinitate," Augustine also grapples with scriptural hermeneutics to affirm his doctrine. Drawing from Genesis, he remarks, "Let us make man in our image, after our likeness" (Gen. 1:26), to indicate the plurality within the Godhead. Augustine argues that the Old Testament hints at the Trinitarian nature of God, which is definitively revealed in the New Testament through Christ and the sending of the Holy Spirit.

Moreover, Augustine's reliance on scripture is not merely exegetical but existential. He believes that every believer can encounter the Trinity within their own experience of faith and community. He illumines this point by referencing Jesus' promise to send the Comforter, the Holy Spirit, to guide believers into all truth (John 16:13). Such passages illustrate Augustine's conviction that God's Trinitarian nature is not an abstract concept but a lived reality, accessible through faith and revelation.

Augustine's Trinitarian theology also speaks to contemporary discussions on divine revelation. For Augustine, the triune God actively communicates to humanity through historical actions and ongoing presence within the Church. This line of thought resonates with the modern theological perspectives of Rahner and von Balthasar, who also grapple with the dynamic unfolding of divine revelation in human history and personal experience.

Beyond scriptural basis, Augustine addresses philosophical objections to the Trinity. Aware of the difficulties in conceptualizing a tri-personal God through human reason, he affirms that divine mystery surpasses human understanding. Nevertheless, he sees philosophical inquiry as valuable, guiding believers to the threshold of faith where revelation completes reason's journey. This harmonizing of faith and reason remains pivotal in Augustine's theological framework.

Central to Augustine's thought is the relational dynamic within the Godhead. He underscores that divine love (caritas) permeates the relationships between Father, Son, and Holy Spirit. This love is not static but dynamic, echoing through creation and incarnating in Jesus Christ's redemptive mission. Augustine finds the highest expression of divine love in Christ's self-giving, reflecting, "Greater love hath no man than this, that a man lay down his life for his friends" (John 15:13).

Through his Trinitarian doctrine, Augustine also addresses the community of believers, urging them to reflect the unity and love of the Trinity in their lives. He envisions the Church as a living body mirroring God's triune nature, bound by love and mutual support. This ecclesiological aspect underscores the practical implications of his theology, advocating for a community grounded in divine, self-giving love.

In conclusion, Augustine's Trinitarian theology serves as a cornerstone for understanding divine revelation. His insights shape not just doctrinal beliefs but the lived faith of the Christian community. By grounding his theology in scripture, philosophically examining it, and unfolding its practical dimensions, Augustine provides a comprehensive vision of the triune God actively revealing Himself in history and in the hearts of believers.

Relevance to Contemporary Understanding of Revelation

St. Augustine's theological framework continues to hold a resonance that transcends centuries, bridging the ancient and the modern in a manner harmonious and profound. His reflections on the Trinitarian nature of God, interwoven with his elucidations on divine revelation, form a bedrock for contemporary theological discourse. To understand Augustine's contributions in light of today's quest for divine knowledge is to recognize an enduring relevancy that speaks to both the heart and intellect.

Augustine's integration of Platonic philosophy with Christian doctrine provides a foundational touchstone for contemporary theologians seeking to harmonize faith and reason. His conceptualization of God as a triune entity—Father, Son, and Holy Spirit—continues to shape modern discourse on the nature of divine revelation. In "Confessions," Augustine's reflections are not merely autobiographical but serve as a nuanced treatise on the human condition and its intrinsic longing for divine truth. "Great art thou, O Lord, and greatly to be praised; great is thy power, and thy wisdom infinite" (Ps. 145:3) echoes a sentiment still deeply pertinent today.

One could argue that Augustine's understanding of the Trinity offers a metaphysical blueprint for contemporary theologians grappling with the complexity of divine revelation in an era marked by rapid scientific and philosophical advancements. His elucidation that the Father, Son, and Holy Spirit are distinct yet indivisible entities provides a model for understanding the unity and diversity of divine acts in history. His insistence on the relational aspect of the Godhead serves as a cornerstone for a relational understanding of revelation today.

In a world increasingly characterized by relativism and skepticism, Augustine's robust defense of objective truth and divine constancy offers a balm. When modern thinkers confront the fluctuating nature of contemporary epistemology, they may find solace in Augustine's assertion that God's nature and revelations are immutable. "For I am the Lord, I change not" (Mal. 3:6), a timeless declaration that Augustine would argue undergirds all divine revelation.

Within Augustine's schema, the act of revelation is also deeply personal, resonating with the existential queries of contemporary believers. Through the lens of his own introspective journey, Augustine demonstrates that revelation is not an abstract, distant event but an intimate, personal encounter. This aspect of revelatory experience finds a parallel in modern existential theology, which seeks to underscore the individuality of divine-human interactions.

Augustine's insights extend beyond the theological to impact contemporary scientific and philosophical dialogues. His notion of 'Confessions' as a form of scientific inquiry into the human soul posits a framework for integrating spirituality with empirical observation. This is strikingly relevant in today's interdisciplinary dialogues where theology and science often intersect, finding common ground in the quest for ultimate truths.

Moreover, Augustine's concept of the 'inner teacher,' the Holy Spirit, as the primary agent of revelation, aligns closely with contemporary focuses on personal spiritual experience. The Spirit's role as the illuminator of divine truths provides a theological basis for understanding modern charismatic movements and personal revelations, often experienced as intimate, transformative encounters.

In light of this, Augustine's teachings act as a bridge between traditional doctrinal formulations and the need for doctrinal development that speaks directly to contemporary challenges. This dynamic relation between perennial truths and modern exigencies is evident in discussions on moral theology, social justice, and ethical dilemmas facing today's Church.

While Augustine might not have confronted issues such as digital ethics, globalized societal structures, or bioethical quandaries, the principles he expounded provide durable tools for addressing such topics. For instance, his emphasis on the primacy of love as the essential characteristic of God's nature offers a moral compass in navigating ethical decisions in an increasingly complex world.

His legacy also persists through liturgical and ecclesial structures that delineate revelation. Augustine's love for sacred Scripture and his exegetical practices continue to inform contemporary scriptural hermeneutics. "All scripture is given by inspiration of God, and is profitable for doctrine, for reproof, for correction, for instruction in righteousness" (2 Tim. 3:16), an assertion that he would heartily affirm, resonates with today's quest to understand divine truth through scriptural study.

Furthermore, Augustine's engagement with the cultural and intellectual currents of his time encourages a similar engagement today. His willingness to dialog with diverse philosophical traditions sets a precedent for theologians who must engage with contemporary intellectual landscapes, ranging from postmodernism to artificial intelligence.

In sum, Augustine's reflections on the Trinity and revelation offer enduring insights that contribute to the contemporary understanding of divine revelation. They serve as a theological and philosophical anchor in the face of modernity's complex challenges. By returning to Augustine, one finds timeless theological wisdom that informs, critiques, and enhances present-day discussions about the nature of God's self-disclosure in our ever-changing world.

Chapter 6: St. Gregory of Nazianzus and the Trinity

Transitioning from the profound insights of St. Augustine, we find ourselves entering the realm of another theological giant: St. Gregory of Nazianzus. Living in the fourth century, Gregory was a key player in the formation and defense of Christian orthodoxy, particularly concerning the Holy Trinity. Alongside his friends and fellow Cappadocian Fathers, Basil the Great and Gregory of Nyssa, Gregory of Nazianzus contributed to a rich theological discourse that continues to influence our understanding of the Triune God.

Gregory's insights into the Trinity are both poetic and philosophical, merging scriptural exegesis with keen philosophical reflection. His approach to the Trinity can best be described as a beautiful symphony, with each Person of the Godhead playing a distinct and harmonious part. Gregory often employed metaphors to elucidate the mystery of the Trinity, describing it as "a single mingling of Light" (Oration 39). This metaphor captures the unity and distinctiveness of the Father, Son, and Holy Spirit.

In his orations, Gregory vehemently defends the consubstantiality of the Son and the Spirit with the Father, aligning with the Nicene Creed's declaration that the Son is "of one essence with the Father" (Nicene Creed). He used Scripture as the backbone of his arguments, emphasizing Jesus' words, "I and my Father are one" (John 10:30). By anchoring his theology in the Bible, Gregory provided a robust defense against Arianism, which denied the full divinity of the Son.

Gregory's theological journey was not merely an academic exercise; it was deeply personal and pastoral. His writings often reflect a man who was acutely aware of the limitations of human language when speaking of God. He once admitted, "What is in us that is like God?" (Oration 28.23), underscoring the profound mystery that the Triune God eludes complete human understanding. Yet, his humility in the face of this mystery did not deter him from attempting to articulate it; rather, it made his contributions all the more profound.

One of Gregory's most significant theological contributions is his articulation of the relationship among the Persons of the Trinity, known as perichoresis, or interpenetration. While the term itself appeared later, the concept is evident in his writings. Gregory illustrated the dynamic relationship within the Trinity by suggesting that the Father, Son, and Holy Spirit exist in a state of mutual indwelling and complete unity. Each Person of the Trinity participates fully in the divine essence without losing individual identity or function.

This concept of perichoresis is not just an abstract idea; it has profound implications for our understanding of community and relationship. If the very nature of God is relational, it follows that human beings, made in the image of God, are called to live in relationships that reflect divine communion. As Gregory stated, "When I say God, I mean Father, Son, and Holy Spirit" (Oration 38.8), urging us to see the relational nature at the core of the divine mystery.

Gregory also tackled the human intellect's struggle with divine concepts. In a profound statement, he noted, "No sooner do I conceive of the One than I am illumined by the splendor of the Three; no sooner do I distinguish them than I am carried back to the One" (Oration 40). This ongoing dialectic captures the tension and beauty of Trinitarian theology, acknowledging both the unity and distinctiveness within the Godhead.

In contemporary times, Gregory's Trinitarian theology offers a robust framework for engaging with modern challenges. His reflections on perichoresis can inform contemporary models of ecclesiology and community life, emphasizing unity without uniformity and diversity without division. Furthermore, his approach to divine mystery invites theologians, scientists, and philosophers alike to approach the study of God with reverence and humility, recognizing the limited capacity of human reason to fully grasp the divine essence.

The modern application of Gregory's theology extends to ecumenical dialogue as well. His emphasis on the consubstantiality of the Trinity provides a common ground for discussions among various Christian traditions. It fosters a spirit of unity based on shared beliefs about the nature of God while allowing for respectful discussions on differences in doctrinal interpretations.

Gregory of Nazianzus's thoughts on the Trinity also encourage a renewed appreciation for the role of the Holy Spirit in the life of believers. He asserted the Spirit's equal divinity and role within the Trinity, as Jesus promised, "But the Comforter, which is the Holy Ghost, whom the Father will send in my name, he shall teach you all things" (John 14:26). In a world frequently marked by division and strife, the Holy Spirit's role as Comforter and Unifier takes on heightened significance.

In conclusion, Gregory of Nazianzus beckons us into a deeper understanding of the divine mystery of the Trinity. His synthesis of scriptural fidelity, philosophical depth, and pastoral sensitivity provides a timeless model for theological reflection. As modern seekers of truth, we too can draw inspiration from Gregory's unwavering commitment to a God who is both incomprehensible and intimately relational. In his words, "It is difficult to conceive God, but to define Him in words is an impossibility...this One of Three and Three of One" (Oration 40),

we find a profound invitation to worship the mystery of the
Triune God.

Gregory's Trinitarian Insights

St. Gregory of Nazianzus, often revered as "The Theologian" in the Eastern Orthodox Church, stands as a beacon of Trinitarian thought. His insights form a rich tapestry that has woven itself into the fabric of Christian theology. Gregory, unlike his contemporaries, delved deeply into the complexities of the Divine, illuminating the mysterious nature of the Trinity with a clarity that was both profound and poetic.

One cannot overstate Gregory's dedication to the articulation of the Trinitarian doctrine. His theological journey was marked by a rigorous defense of the consubstantiality of the Father, Son, and Holy Spirit. Gregory's orations, particularly the celebrated "Theological Orations," reflect his mastery in navigating the perilous waters between Arianism and Modalism. He stood firm in the affirmation that the Father, Son, and Holy Spirit are distinct yet of one essence. This principle, encapsulated in the term *homoousios*, was poignantly articulated during the First Council of Constantinople in 381.

Gregory's language is drenched in a poetry of paradox. He acknowledges the difficulty of speaking about God without falling into theological error. In this way, Gregory anticipates the modern understanding of apophatic theology—the idea that God's true essence is beyond human comprehension. Yet,

Gregory does not settle for agnosticism about God's nature; instead, he strives to balance divine incomprehensibility with the revelation available to finite human minds. As he says, "No sooner do I conceive of the One than I am illumined by the splendor of the Three; no sooner do I distinguish them than I am carried back to the One" (Oration 40.41).

Such expressions underscore the dynamic tension in Gregory's theology. While the Father is the source of the Trinity, He is never alone. The Son is eternally begotten, and the Holy Spirit eternally proceeds. Gregory firmly adheres to Scriptural testimony to support these views, often invoking passages such as Matthew 28:19, where Jesus commands His disciples to baptize "in the name of the Father, and of the Son, and of the Holy Ghost" (Matt. 28:19). This Trinitarian formula not only provides a basis for understanding the relational distinctions within the Godhead but also grounds his theology in the praxis of the early Church.

Furthermore, Gregory's insights extend beyond mere doctrinal formulations. He explores the implications of the Trinity for Christian life and spirituality. He emphasizes the idea that the believer's experience of God mirrors the relational dynamics of the Trinity. Each person of the Trinity has a role in the believer's journey: the Father as Creator, the Son as Redeemer, and the Holy Spirit as Sanctifier. This experiential dimension is crucial for understanding the transformative power of Trinitarian doctrine. Gregory asserts that the process of becoming more like God, known as *theosis* or divinization, involves participating in the divine life of the Trinity. In essence, to be in communion with one Person of the Trinity is to be in communion with all three.

Gregory uses numerous metaphors to illuminate these relationships. He describes the Trinity as a "triad of light" or as three suns sharing a single light, emphasizing unity and distinction. These metaphors are not mere literary flourishes but are central to Gregory's theological method. They assist in understanding the mystery of the Trinity without reducing it to simplistic categories. In another metaphor, Gregory likens the relationship between the Trinity to the roots, trunk, and branches of a tree, showing how they are both distinct and one.

The theological method of Gregory is both contemplative and pastoral. He challenges the Church to engage deeply with the mystery of the Trinity, urging that this engagement is not just for intellectual fulfillment but for spiritual transformation. Gregory's teachings urge believers to see the world through a Trinitarian lens, where love and relationality are foundational to all existence. His reflections serve as a bridge between doctrinal orthodoxy and the lived experience of the divine.

Gregory's emphasis on the unity and distinction within the Trinity also has significant implications for modern theological discourse. In an age where individualism often overshadows communal identity, Gregory's insights remind us that true personhood is found in relationship. His Trinitarian model offers a counter-narrative to contemporary fragmentation, advocating for a vision of unity that embraces diversity without erasing difference. This is particularly relevant in ecumenical dialogues, where understanding and accepting theological nuances among different denominations and traditions remain crucial.

Additionally, Gregory's focus on the Holy Spirit is of particular interest for modern pneumatology. At a time when the role of the Spirit is being rediscovered in various Christian traditions, Gregory's balanced and robust Trinitarian framework provides a rich resource. He emphasizes the Spirit's role in both individual transformation and the life of the Church, articulating a pneumatology that is deeply interwoven with both Christology and ecclesiology.

In conclusion, St. Gregory of Nazianzus offers profound insights into the mystery of the Trinity that continue to resonate in modern theological discussions. His ability to maintain the delicate balance between the unity and distinctiveness of the divine persons provides a model for both theological reflection and spiritual practice. As we navigate the complexities of contemporary faith, Gregory's theology invites us to explore the depths of divine mystery with both reverence and intellect. His contributions serve as a vital reminder that understanding the Trinity is not an academic exercise but a journey into the heart of God, shaping how we live and relate to one another.

Through his meticulous articulation of Trinitarian doctrine, Gregory provides a timeless gift to the Church, enabling a deeper communion with the Father, Son, and Holy Spirit. His insights form an essential part of the foundation upon which the edifice of Christian theology is built, inviting each generation to engage anew with the profound mystery of the Triune God.

Modern Applications of Gregory's Theology

In the modern landscape, St. Gregory of Nazianzus's theological writings hold more than historical interest; they serve as a live conduit to the deeper understanding of the Triune God. Gregory, a Cappadocian Father, has left us with a rich tapestry of thought that bears relevance to contemporary theological discourse. His preoccupation with the Trinity is far from archaic; in fact, it speaks powerfully to the challenges and questions posed by modern believers and skeptics alike. Thus, Gregory's theological framework can be applied to various modern contexts, ranging from ecclesial praxis to interfaith dialogue.

In his seminal work on the Trinity, Gregory emphasizes the distinct persons yet consubstantial essence of the Father, Son, and Holy Spirit. This understanding can offer modern believers a nuanced perspective in addressing the mystery of divine unity and diversity. The societal obsession with individualism often distances people from communal and relational aspects. Gregory's theology reminds us that individuality is not eradicated in unity but finds its true expression within it. "For there are three that bear record in heaven, the Father, the Word, and the Holy Ghost: and these three are one" (1 John 5:7). This Trinitarian ethos promotes a model wherein community and individuality coalesce harmoniously.

Moreover, Gregory's articulation of divine revelation through the Son and the Spirit is profoundly applicable to modern interdenominational and interreligious discussions. His idea that the Word becomes incarnate and the Spirit enlightens can be seen as a precursor to theologies that emphasize God's ongoing self-disclosure in history and culture. This dynamic of revelation, through both tangible and intangible means, can aid theologians in fostering dialogues with non-Christian faith traditions. Gregory provides a robust framework for understanding that the revelation is not static but an ongoing, relational process.

On a practical ecclesiastical level, Gregory's sermons present a compelling guide for modern homiletics. His oratory, rich in scriptural exegesis and rhetorical flourish, remains an exemplary model for those preaching in today's parlance. He argues for a balance between doctrinal precision and pastoral care, a balance that is essential for contemporary clergy who must navigate the turbulent waters of theological complexities while meeting the pastoral needs of their congregations. His insistence on the pastoral responsibility of theological accuracy holds today's preachers accountable to a standard that is both intellectually rigorous and spiritually nourishing.

A constructive alignment of Gregory's Trinitarian theology can also be seen in contemporary sacramental theology. Sacraments are understood as manifestations of divine grace mediated through material means—the incarnational principle Gregory so ardently defended. The Eucharist, in particular, can be viewed through the lens of Gregory's thought. It embodies the unity of the divine and the human, a locus where Christ's sacrificial love meets human redemption. "This is my body, which is broken for you: this do in remembrance of me" (1 Cor. 11:24). His teachings impress upon modern Catholic liturgical practice the gravity and mystery of the sacraments.

In the realm of ethics, Gregory's Trinitarian insights have profound implications. He posits that ethical life is rooted in the imitation of divine life, specifically the relational dynamics within the Trinity. Modern bioethics, social justice teachings, and environmental stewardship can all draw from this well. The communal love witnessed in the Trinity provides a model for altruistic human interaction and global solidarity. Thus, Gregory's theology of the Trinity becomes a template for ethical behavior that extends beyond mere moralism to encompass a holistic vision of human flourishing in communion with God and neighbor.

Furthermore, Gregory's theology addresses the existential anxieties of the modern individual. His poetic expressions of the divine mysteries offer a counter-narrative to the often fragmented modern self. These poetic articulations invite believers to see their lives as stories interwoven with the divine narrative. His reflections on the human condition—fraught with sin yet destined for divine communion—provide solace and a sense of purpose. The modern individual, often caught in a web of existential doubts, can find in Gregory's writings a reassuring voice that calls for both introspection and transcendence.

The implications of Gregory's theology also extend into the political sphere. His understanding of the Trinity invites a reevaluation of authority and community. Authority, as mirrored in the relationality of the divine persons, is not about domination but about mutual love and service. This has profound implications for how we understand leadership and governance in both religious and secular spheres. Gregory offers a vision where power is exercised not as coercion but as an act of self-giving love.

Lastly, Gregory's emphasis on the Holy Spirit can also nurture contemporary pneumatology. Gregory describes the Spirit as the source of life and sanctification, emphasizing the Spirit's role in both personal and communal transformation. In a world increasingly plagued by secularization and spiritual apathy, his insights draw attention to the necessity and presence of the Spirit in vivifying the Church and its mission. The Spirit's work in the sacraments, charismatic gifts, and everyday Christian living reminds modern believers that they are always in the dynamic presence of God, constantly called to holiness and renewal. "And be not drunk with wine, wherein is excess; but be filled with the Spirit" (Eph. 5:18).

St. Gregory of Nazianzus offers a robust theological edifice that is not only historically significant but also perpetually insightful for contemporary issues. His Trinitarian theology serves as a lens through which the modern Church can view and address a myriad of spiritual, ethical, and existential concerns. By engaging deeply with Gregory's thought, we are reminded that ancient wisdom can illuminate modern challenges, and that the eternal truths of the Trinity continue to offer profound insights for the life and mission of the Church today.

Chapter 7: Trinitarian Theology: Augustine vs. Gregory

In the rich tapestry of Christian thought, the theology of the Trinity stands as a vital, albeit complex, doctrine. Two figures loom large in its development: Augustine of Hippo and Gregory of Nazianzus. Both sought to unravel the divine mystery of the Trinity, though their approaches and interpretations provide distinct lenses through which we can view the same profound truth.

Augustine's trinitarian theology is characterized by his profound emphasis on the inner life of God. Influenced by Neo-Platonism, Augustine approached the mystery of the Trinity through the lens of psychological analogies. He famously drew parallels between the Trinity and the human mind, using the triad of memory, understanding, and will as a reflection of the divine tri-unity. "For there are three that bear record in heaven, the Father, the Word, and the Holy Ghost: and these three are one" (1 John 5:7). Augustine probed into the depths of this oneness, emphasizing the relational aspect within the Godhead, a unity of love that binds the persons together.

In contrast, Gregory of Nazianzus approached the Trinity with a strong emphasis on the distinctiveness of the three Persons. Known for his Cappadocian background, Gregory refuted any subordination within the Trinity, stressing instead the co-equal and co-eternal nature of the Father, Son, and Holy Spirit. He argued that while each person of the Trinity is fully God, each has distinctive roles that are not interchangeable. "Go ye therefore, and teach all nations, baptizing them in the name of the Father, and of the Son, and of the Holy Ghost" (Matt. 28:19). For Gregory, this mandate highlighted the distinct yet unified identities in the divine mission.

Their differing approaches lead us to a broader understanding of the Trinity itself. Augustine's framework tends to be more introspective, focusing on the internal relations within the Godhead. His psychological analogy brings a more intimate perspective, presenting the Trinity as reflective of the complexities within the human soul. This internalization is crucial for personal spirituality, offering believers a way to contemplate God's nature within themselves.

On the other hand, Gregory's emphasis on the distinctiveness of the Persons provided a critical defense against heresies such as Modalism and Arianism. By underscoring the individuality within the Godhead, Gregory preserved the diversity of divine operations—each person acting uniquely yet in concert with the other two. This focus on the exterior distinctions of the Trinity stresses the relational and communal nature of God, thus encouraging believers to see the importance of community and relational integrity in their own lives.

The theological implications of their views extend far beyond their respective eras. Augustine's vision fosters an inward journey that builds a bridge between the divine and the human psyche, allowing a transformative union of the believer's soul with God. His influence is seen in the thought patterns of countless theologians who followed, from Aquinas to Rahner. Conversely, Gregory's clarity on the distinctions within the Trinity laid essential groundwork for later ecclesiastical definitions, influencing the outcomes of pivotal councils such as Chalcedon and influencing Eastern Orthodox theology significantly.

Reconciling these perspectives reveals a multifaceted doctrine that is both a mystery to be contemplated and a reality to be lived. Augustine and Gregory's contributions are complementary rather than contradictory. Together, they provide a more comprehensive view of the Trinity: one that integrates both relational intimacy and distinct personhood. "Hear, O Israel: The LORD our God is one LORD" (Deut. 6:4) juxtaposed with "And the Word was made flesh, and dwelt among us" (John 1:14) evokes a full spectrum of theological depth, from oneness in essence to distinctiveness in action.

As contemporary theologians and believers seek to understand the mysteries of the divine, both Augustine and Gregory offer invaluable insights. Augustine invites us to delve into the internal experience of God's triune nature—a meditative journey within our own souls. Gregory, however, calls us outward, to recognize and honor the distinct roles and relationships inherent within the Trinity, drawing us into communal and relational authenticity. Their legacies compel us to explore both dimensions to grasp the full reality of the God we worship.

In sum, Augustine and Gregory's theological endeavors provide us with a more nuanced and holistic understanding of the Trinity. By appreciating both the shared substance and distinct persons of the Trinity, we are better equipped to engage in both personal devotion and communal worship. Their teachings remind us that the mystery of God's nature is not solely a doctrinal assertion but a living truth that should inform every aspect of our lives. Through Augustine's introspection and Gregory's emphasis on relational dynamics, we can see a divine harmony that invites us into deeper communion with the Triune God.

Recognizing the immense contributions of these two theological giants, we position ourselves to explore and experience the full spectrum of the Trinity's revelation. Their diverse yet complementary perspectives encourage us to embrace a faith that is both intellectually robust and spiritually enriching, a reflection of the endless depth of the Godhead itself. In this way, the dual lenses of Augustine and Gregory provide a clearer and richer vision of divine reality, ever inviting believers to a fuller participation in the life and love of the Triune God.

Detailed Comparisons

When exploring the theological thought of St. Augustine and St. Gregory of Nazianzus on the Trinity, one is invited into a deep well of contemplation and reverence, echoing the profound mysteries they sought to unravel. Each theologian, with his unique lens, brought forth intricate understandings and towering expositions that have profoundly influenced the Christian doctrine of the Triune God.

Augustine, a Bishop of Hippo, approached the Trinity with the mind of a philosopher and the heart of a pastor. He famously utilized analogies derived from human experience, particularly the human mind, to elucidate the divine mysteries. Gregory, a Cappadocian Father, embraced a more mystical and liturgical approach, emphasizing the experiences of divine worship and the ineffable nature of God. While both theologians upheld the co-equality and co-eternity of the Father, Son, and Holy Spirit, their methodologies and emphases distinguished them significantly.

The comparative analysis between Augustine and Gregory brings to light Augustine's relational model within the Godhead, often termed the psychological model. In his seminal work *De Trinitate*, Augustine proposed that the human mind's memory, understanding, and will provide an apt, though imperfect,

analogy for understanding the Trinity. Each of these faculties, while distinct, operates in a unified manner, reflecting the inner dynamics of the Triune God. As Augustine posited, "These three are one, and each in itself is one also."
(Augustine, De Trinitate 10.10.14)

In contrast, Gregory of Nazianzus pursued a more apophatic theology—a theology of what cannot be said about God. Gregory employed the language of mystery and paradox to articulate his insights into the Trinitarian life. This mystical approach is augmented in his *Orations*, where he evocatively describes the incomprehensible light of the Trinity: "No sooner do I conceive of the One than I am illumined by the splendour of the Three; no sooner do I distinguish Them than I am carried back to the One."
(Gregory of Nazianzus, Oratio 40.41)

Where Augustine leaned heavily into philosophical reasoning, Gregory emphasized the importance of doxological context—liturgy and prayer—as the primary arena for encountering and reflecting on the Triune God. This distinction becomes crucial as we consider the broader implications of their respective theologies for modern revelation. Augustine's analogical method lends itself to a more systematic theology, whereas Gregory's liturgical approach offers a theology profoundly rooted in the mysticism of worship.

The disparity in their approaches can be grounded further in their differing contexts and backgrounds. Augustine's intellectual environment was deeply infused with Neo-Platonism, which shaped his ability to see analogies between the divine and human nature. Gregory, on the other hand, was more influenced by the traditions of Eastern Christianity, with its rich liturgical life and a greater emphasis on theosis or divinization. These backgrounds not only informed their theological projects but also hinted at the diverse ways in which the Church has historically encountered the mystery of God.

Moreover, their different methodologies have left distinctive marks on how subsequent generations have engaged with the doctrine of the Trinity. Augustine's analogical reasoning finds resonance in Western theological tradition, where reason and rational discourse often occupy the theological center stage. On the flip side, Gregory's emphasis on the ineffability of God and the centrality of worship continues to enrich Eastern Orthodox theology, which prioritizes the mysteries and sacramental life.

Another salient point of comparison lies in their respective use of scriptural exegesis. Augustine's exegesis, deeply allegorical, was intrinsic to his Trinitarian thought. His interpretation of John 1:1 ("In the beginning was the Word, and the Word was with God, and the Word was God.") serves as a foundational text, intricately woven into his theology to elucidate the relationships within the Trinity and the incarnation of Christ. For Augustine, the Word's becoming flesh was an integral part of his understanding of divine revelation and the communication of God's love to humanity.

Gregory, while also scripturally rooted, displayed a proclivity for integrating scriptural contemplation with the living tradition of the Church. His exegetical method was less concerned with allegory and more with a meditative and prayerful reflection, often bringing out the liturgical and sacramental dimensions of the text. This can be observed in his treatment of passages like Matthew 28:19 ("Go ye therefore, and teach all nations, baptizing them in the name of the Father, and of the Son, and of the Holy Ghost.")—an affirmation of the trinitarian formula deeply embedded in the church's sacramental practice. For Gregory, the scriptural mandate to baptize in the name of the Trinity was not only theological but profoundly liturgical.

Despite their differences, both theologians affirmed the consubstantiality, co-eternity, and co-equality of the Divine Persons. They both vehemently opposed Arianism, upholding the full divinity of the Son and the Spirit. Augustine and Gregory reinforced the Nicene Creed's declarations, establishing a theological bulwark against heresies that sought to divide or diminish the Godhead.

Their divergences are thus wrapped within a greater symphony of theological unity, a testament to the richness and depth of the Christian tradition's encounter with the living God. Augustine's intellectually rigorous exposition complements Gregory's mystical and worship-oriented approach, offering the faithful varied yet harmonious pathways to engage with the Triune God.

In the modern context, Augustine's psychological analogy and Gregory's liturgical mysticism offer interpretative tools that remain relevant for contemporary theological discourse. Augustine's approach can aid discussions within philosophical theology, providing a framework to engage the rationality of faith. Gregory's profound liturgical insights can rejuvenate the sacramental life of the Church, inspiring a deeper sense of the mystical presence of God in worship.

Their theological legacies, while distinct, converge in the shared belief in a God who reveals Himself as a communion of Persons. This Triune God enters human history, drawing us into the divine life through grace. As modern theologians, philosophers, and scientists continue to explore these ancient yet ever-relevant truths, the insights of Augustine and Gregory act as both foundation and beacon, guiding the faithful deeper into the mystery of divine love and revelation. Thus, the comparative study of their trinitarian theology not only enriches our historical understanding but also invites us into a continuing journey of faith and discovery.

Broader Theological Implications

The examination of Trinitarian theology through the lenses of Augustine and Gregory reveals a complex interplay of divine revelation, human understanding, and theological interpretation. Their perspectives, while rooted in the early centuries of the Church, offer enduring insights relevant to contemporary theological discourse. At the heart of this exploration lies a profound question: How does the nature of the Triune God shape our understanding of revelation and its implications for modern faith practice?

In Augustine's writings, particularly in "De Trinitate," we encounter a profound reflection on the unity and distinctions within the Godhead. His analogy of the mind, memory, and will provides a framework for understanding how God can be three distinct persons yet one essence. Augustine's use of psychological analogies opens avenues for contemporary theologians to explore the immanent and economic dimensions of God's being. For Augustine, the Trinity is not just a doctrinal formula but a dynamic reality that influences every aspect of Christian life and worship. Such an understanding compels us to see revelation not merely as intellectual assent but as an experiential encounter with the living God.

Gregory of Nazianzus, on the other hand, emphasizes the mystery and ineffability of the Trinity, cautioning against overconfidence in human reason to comprehend divine realities. His poetic and often paradoxical language underscores the limitations of human speech when faced with the Divine Mystery. Gregory's approach invites modern theologians to embrace a sense of wonder and humility in the face of God's Self-revelation. In the words of Paul, "For now we see through a glass, darkly; but then face to face: now I know in part; but then shall I know even as also I am known" (1 Cor. 13:12). Gregory's insistence on the apophatic way, or the via negativa, serves as a counterbalance to the kataphatic theology that seeks to articulate God's nature positively and precisely.

The convergence of Augustine and Gregory's thoughts on the Trinity demands a holistic approach to theology, one that synthesizes reason and mystery. Augustine's intellectual rigor coupled with Gregory's mystical reverence forms a comprehensive framework for understanding the Triune God. This synthesis has profound implications for other areas of theology, such as Christology, soteriology, and ecclesiology. For instance, the relational dynamics within the Trinity provide a model for human relationships, both within the church and the broader community. The love and unity within the Godhead become the paradigm for Christian love and fellowship.

Moreover, the Trinitarian doctrines of Augustine and Gregory challenge and inform our understanding of divine revelation itself. Revelation, in this context, is seen not merely as the communication of propositional truths but as the self-disclosure of a relational God. This relational dimension emphasizes that revelation is not static but dynamic, involving an ongoing interaction between God and humanity. Just as the Trinity exists in a state of eternal relation, so too does revelation unfold in the context of a living relationship between the Creator and creation. This idea resonates with the biblical notion that "the Spirit itself beareth witness with our spirit, that we are the children of God" (Rom. 8:16).

The implications extend to how we read and interpret Scripture. Augustine's hermeneutical principles, grounded in the love of God and neighbor, require us to approach biblical texts with a view to fostering genuine Christian love and unity. Gregory's focus on the mystical and contemplative offers an additional layer, urging believers to seek the deeper, often hidden, meanings within the Sacred Writings. Together, these approaches encourage a reading of Scripture that is both intellectually rigorous and spiritually enriching, aiming to transform the reader's heart as well as mind.

In considering these broader implications, one might turn to the modern theological landscape where thinkers like Karl Rahner and Hans Urs von Balthasar have advanced Trinitarian theology in ways that align with the foundational ideas of Augustine and Gregory. Rahner's famous axiom that the "economic Trinity is the immanent Trinity, and vice versa" echoes Augustine's insight into the inseparability of God's actions in history and God's eternal nature. Von Balthasar's dramatization of the Trinitarian relationships offers a bold and creative way to engage with the implications of divine revelation for contemporary culture and spirituality.

Rahner's theology emphasizes that our understanding of God must always be rooted in the historical revelation of Jesus Christ and the ongoing experience of the Holy Spirit in the Church. This perspective aligns with Augustine's profound reflection on the historical and communal dimensions of revelation. Rahner's concept of the "anonymous Christian," suggesting that God's grace operating outside explicit Christian boundaries, finds a counterpoint in Augustine's more exclusivist stance yet opens a dialogue about the universality of salvation—a topic that Gregory might approach with a sense of reverent mystery.

Von Balthasar, with his focus on beauty and aesthetics, brings to light the experiential and sensory dimensions of revelation, reminiscent of Gregory's poetic theology. He contends that the glory of God revealed in Christ is not only a truth to be understood but a beauty to be experienced and lived. This aesthetic dimension provides a new lens through which to view Augustine's and Gregory's theological contributions, emphasizing that the Truth of God is also the Beauty of God, leading believers to a deeper, more holistic form of worship and discipleship.

Thus, the broader theological implications of Augustine and Gregory's Trinitarian theology resonate deeply with the questions and challenges of modern theological reflection. Their approaches compel us to navigate the tension between knowledge and mystery, reason and experience, doctrine and life. As we engage with their thought, we find ourselves drawn into a deeper understanding of the relational and dynamic nature of divine revelation. Their insights encourage us to contemplate the mystery of the Triune God with both intellectual rigor and humble awe, affirming that true knowledge of God entails not just knowing about Him but entering into communion with Him.

In conclusion, the study of Augustine and Gregory of Nazianzus articulates a Trinitarian theology rich with potential for ongoing theological inquiry and spiritual growth. It challenges contemporary theologians, philosophers, scientists, and believers to integrate their intellectual pursuits with a lived experience of the divine mystery. The Triune God revealed through their writings calls us to a deeper, more transformative encounter with His self-revelation, one that shapes our understanding of faith, community, and the universe itself. This understanding beckons us to echo the psalmist's timeless invitation: "O taste and see that the Lord is good: blessed is the man that trusteth in him" (Ps. 34:8).

Chapter 8: Blessed Elena GuerraÃ¢ÂÂs Teachings

Bearing witness to divine revelations requires us to lend an ear to the voices of those who have walked closely with the Holy Spirit. One such voice from contemporary times is that of Blessed Elena Guerra. Her teachings fuse the mystical with the practical, offering insights that enrich our understanding of modern revelation.

Blessed Elena Guerra, born in Lucca, Italy in the 19th century, devoted her life to invoking a renewed outpouring of the Holy Spirit. She is often associated with the Pentecostal renewal within the Roman Catholic Church, deeply convinced that the faithful needed to reconnect with the experiences of the early Christians. Her focus on Pentecost was not merely a historical curiosity but a spiritual clarion call to the modern Church.

It was through her letters to Pope Leo XIII that Elena emphasized the importance of the Holy Spirit's role in the life of every believer. "Revive in the Church, O Lord, the Spirit of Pentecost," she wrote, urging the Pope to dedicate more attention to the Third Person of the Holy Trinity. Her zeal was akin to that which is written: "And when the day of Pentecost was fully come, they were all with one accord in one place" (Acts 2:1). Elena's vision was to see the Church once again united and spirited, alive with divine fire.

What makes Guerra's insights particularly striking is her belief that every Christian has the capacity to receive direct inspiration from the Holy Spirit, a belief that shifted the theological landscape of her time. She introduced a renewed focus on personal holiness and communal prayer, continuously harking back to the New Testament's promises about the Paraclete. "But the Comforter, which is the Holy Ghost, whom the Father will send in my name, he shall teach you all things" (John 14:26).

Her role in modern revelation cannot be understated. Elena Guerra pushed for the Church to expect and experience the supernatural in everyday life. Her teachings not only fostered a deeper desire for spiritual gifts among the laity but also reaffirmed the charismatic nature of the early Church. Her influence extended well beyond her earthly life, leading to the establishment of numerous prayer groups and renewal movements. These groups continue to thrive, perpetuating her fervent plea for a spiritually vibrant Church.

For the modern theologian, Guerra's teachings beckon a return to a lived, dynamic faith. They challenge the often sterile academic discourse about revelation, reminding us that divine truths cannot be confined to intellectual paradigms alone. Instead, they are to be lived out in the experience of the Holy Spirit's continued movement and guidance. This aspect resonates with Scriptural exhortations: "Quench not the Spirit. Despise not prophesyings" (1 Thess. 5:19-20).

Thus, the teachings of Elena Guerra invite a balanced approach to theology—a blend of rigorous intellectual inquiry and supernatural expectation. She embodies the vision of a faith that is both deeply historical and startlingly present. Her focus on Pentecost, far from being a relic of the past, is a call to anticipate and experience ongoing revelation.

Moreover, Guerra's commitment to personal sanctity and community prayer offers practical frameworks for experiencing this revelation. Her encouragement to pray for the gifts of the Spirit aligns seamlessly with Paul's teachings: "But covet earnestly the best gifts: and yet shew I unto you a more excellent way" (1 Cor. 12:31). Through prayer, study, and openness to the Spirit, contemporary believers are invited into a deeper, more vibrant relationship with God.

One of Elena's most profound impacts was her ability to translate deep theological truths into lived experiences. Her teachings bridge the gap between theology and spirituality, making divine mysteries accessible and experiential. This approach dismantles the misconception that mystical experiences are reserved for the few, highlighting instead that the Holy Spirit's gifts are available to all who earnestly seek them.

As we consider the implications of her teachings for our modern understanding of revelation, it's crucial to recognize her contributions to the larger theological discourse. Guerra's focus on the Holy Spirit's role offers a nuanced view that complements and enriches the perspectives of Augustinian, Rahnerian, and Balthasarian thought. Each theologian, in their unique way, underscores different dimensions of God's revelation, and Guerra's emphasis on Pentecost ties these insights into a cohesive whole.

In essence, Blessed Elena Guerra's teachings serve as a clarion call for renewal—a plea for the Church to embrace the fullness of the Holy Spirit in its journey toward holiness and mission. Her life and legacy remind us that revelation is not a static event of the past but a dynamic, ongoing encounter with the Divine, urging the faithful to remain open, expectant, and fervent.

As we delve deeper into the study of modern revelation, let us be inspired by Guerra's unwavering faith and her fervent desire for a Church enlivened by the Holy Spirit. Her teachings are a testament to the power of prayer, the importance of unity, and the ever-present guidance of the Paraclete. May we, too, seek to know God more intimately, as she did, and allow the Spirit to lead us into all truth.

Elena Guerra's Focus on Pentecost

Blessed Elena Guerra's teachings are deeply anchored in the transformative event of Pentecost. Her focus on this significant event in the Christian liturgical calendar reveals a mystical yet practical approach to understanding the perpetual action of the Holy Spirit in the life of the believer and the Church. Pentecost, as described in the Acts of the Apostles, marks the commencement of the Church's mission to evangelize all nations. Guerra stressed that this mission, empowered by the Holy Spirit, remains as essential now as it was in the early Church. "And when the day of Pentecost was fully come, they were all with one accord in one place" (Acts 2:1). Through such scriptural lens, Guerra sees Pentecost not as a distant historical event, but as a continual outpouring of the Spirit.

Guerra's emphasis on Pentecost brings to mind the unity and communal aspect pivotal to the early Church. When the Holy Spirit descended upon the disciples, it wasn't just an individual experience but a collective one, signifying the beginning of a universal mission. This collective outpouring signifies the inclusivity and the breadth of the Church's mission. Through her meditations and exhortations, Guerra continually urged the faithful to embrace this communal and missionary spirit, emphasizing the role of the Holy Spirit in guiding and uniting the Church. Her writings often reflect the vibrant, communal energy witnessed during Pentecost, seeking to recreate that fervor in the modern age.

In a time marked by rampant individualism, Guerra's focus on Pentecost calls the faithful back to a sense of communal calling and shared mission. She believed that every believer is part of the ongoing Pentecost, equipped by the Holy Spirit to bear witness to the truth of the Gospel. This continuous action of the Spirit is what she saw as essential for renewing the Church and invigorating its mission in the world. Just as the early disciples were emboldened to speak in various tongues and proclaim the good news, modern-day Christians, according to Guerra, are similarly empowered to address the contemporary challenges of faith. "And they were all filled with the Holy Ghost, and began to speak with other tongues, as the Spirit gave them utterance" (Acts 2:4).

Pentecost, for Guerra, was also a profound reminder of the fulfillment of Christ's promise to send an Advocate. This promise is encapsulated in the words of Jesus: "But the Comforter, which is the Holy Ghost, whom the Father will send in my name, he shall teach you all things, and bring all things to your remembrance, whatsoever I have said unto you" (John 14:26). Guerra's reflections draw heavily on this assurance, urging a return to a fervent recognition of the Holy Spirit's active presence and role in personal sanctification and the collective edification of the Church.

Fostering a deeper devotion to the Holy Spirit, as Guerra proposed, involves a conscious openness to divine inspiration. She called for an intimate relationship with the Holy Spirit, marked by prayer, discernment, and receptivity to the Spirit's gifts. It is within this relational dynamic that Guerra believed the Church would find the wisdom and courage necessary to confront contemporary spiritual and social issues. In her spiritual correspondence, she frequently exhorted her contemporaries to seek the Holy Spirit's guidance in all endeavors, recognizing that human effort alone is insufficient for divine works.

Guerra's Pentecostal emphasis also intertwined with her Marian devotion. She pointed out that the Blessed Virgin Mary was present with the apostles at Pentecost, embodying the perfect recipient of the Holy Spirit's outpouring. This Marian aspect of Pentecost underscores the role of Mary as the Mother of the Church and the model disciple, perfectly attuned to the Spirit's movements. This connection encouraged the faithful to seek Mary's intercession and example in their own spiritual lives, aspiring to the same openness and fidelity to the Spirit demonstrated by her.

Furthermore, Guerra insisted on the enduring need for a "new Pentecost" in the life of the Church. By this, she did not mean a repetition of the original event, but a renewed openness to the Spirit that could invigorate the Church's mission in every age. This idea resonates with the theological concept of "ecclesia semper reformanda," the Church always in need of renewal. Guerra's call for a new Pentecost invites believers to continuously seek the Spirit's renewal in their lives, thus ensuring that the Church remains vibrant, dynamic, and responsive to the needs of the world.

Her correspondence with Pope Leo XIII, who subsequently initiated various prayers invoking the Holy Spirit, reflects how her teachings on Pentecost had a significant impact on contemporary ecclesial practices. Guerra's influence illustrates how personal piety and devotion can lead to broader ecclesiastical reforms and deepen the Church's understanding and experience of divine mysteries. It exemplifies the interplay between individual spirituality and institutional practice, showcasing how the fervent faith of one individual can ripple through the ecclesial structure.

In practice, Guerra's focus on Pentecost encourages a lived experience of the Holy Spirit that goes beyond mere theological reflection. Her teachings challenge believers to cultivate a dynamic relationship with the Spirit, engaging in acts of love, justice, and mercy as concrete expressions of the Spirit's presence and action in the world. The Holy Spirit, being the source of all charisms and ministries, mobilizes the faithful to diverse forms of service and witness, reflecting the manifold dimensions of Pentecost's gift. "Now there are diversities of gifts, but the same Spirit" (1 Corinthians 12:4).

To encapsulate, Blessed Elena Guerra's focus on Pentecost illuminates a path for contemporary believers to experience and witness the living presence of the Holy Spirit actively. Her teachings urge a communal, continual receptiveness to the Spirit's guidance, emphasizing renewal, unity, and dynamic mission within the Church. Guerra's vision implores the faithful to a deeper devotion to the Holy Spirit, fostering an ever-renewing Pentecostal flame that sustains the transformative mission of the Church in every age.

Her Role in Modern Revelation

Blessed Elena Guerra occupies a distinctive position within the panorama of modern revelation through her unique focus on the Holy Spirit and divine inspiration. In an age where the pneumatic movements of the Spirit might appear overshadowed by rationalistic approaches, Guerra's teachings reverberate with a call to rekindle the sense of divine immanence. "For where two or three are gathered together in my name, there am I in the midst of them" (Matt. 18:20), Guerra underscores the palpable presence of the Divine in communal and personal spheres. Her emphasis is a clarion call to a new Pentecost, rejuvenating the Church and individual believers alike.

In her tireless advocacy for the Holy Spirit's enlivening force, Guerra serves as a nexus between the apostolic era and contemporary times. Her messages stress the necessity to experience a personal Pentecost, a transformative encounter with the Divine Spirit. This parallels the biblical imagery: "And suddenly there came a sound from heaven as of a rushing mighty wind, and it filled all the house where they were sitting" (Acts 2:2). Guerra exhorts that such spiritually dramatic experiences should not be relics of the past but vibrant realities of the present age.

Guerra's writings and exhortations are rich with a theological and mystical tapestry that underscores a living, dynamic revelation. In a manner reminiscent of von Balthasar's dramatic theology, Guerra paints a vibrant portrait of a God who is actively involved in the mundane moments, not confined to sacred spaces alone. She contends that the Spirit is a constant companion, intimately involved in the facets of human life, echoing the biblical truth, "But the Comforter, which is the Holy Ghost, whom the Father will send in my name, he shall teach you all things, and bring all things to your remembrance, whatsoever I have said unto you" (John 14:26).

The theological contributions of Guerra are not merely theoretical but have profound practical implications for the believer's life. Her teachings call for an active and responsive faith, urging individuals to seek the Holy Spirit with fervor and expect divine intervention in worldly affairs. This expectation aligns with the Pauline view, "For as many as are led by the Spirit of God, they are the sons of God" (Rom. 8:14), proposing that modern revelation is accessible and transformative through the immediate presence and guidance of the Holy Spirit.

This modern revelation, as espoused by Guerra, pivots on the personal encounter—where the human spirit meets the Divine Spirit through prayer, meditation, and sacraments. Guerra encourages a contemplative yet active spirituality that stays aligned with traditional teachings while dynamically engaging the contemporary context. Her role, therefore, is akin to that of a spiritual conduit, facilitating a continuously unfolding revelation that meets the timely needs of an ever-evolving Church.

Elena Guerra's advocacy also extends to the communal dimension of revelation. She insists that a renewed outpouring of the Holy Spirit begins within the heart of the faith community, reflecting the early church's practice of communal prayer and devotion. "These all continued with one accord in prayer and supplication, with the women, and Mary the mother of Jesus, and with his brethren" (Acts 1:14). Guerra's teachings transform these early Christian practices into imperatives for modern ecclesial life, urging a collective pursuit of spiritual renewal.

Invoking the Holy Spirit is central to understanding Guerra's role in contemporary theological discourse on revelation. Her teachings underscore that true knowledge of God is continually revealed through the Spirit and accessible to all who earnestly seek it. This democratizing aspect of revelation stands as a counterpoint to the elitist perceptions often associated with divine knowledge, asserting that "the manifestation of the Spirit is given to every man to profit withal" (1 Cor. 12:7).

By emphasizing the universality of the Holy Spirit's work, Guerra inspires a broader, more inclusive theology of revelation.

She argues that every individual, irrespective of their ecclesiastical standing, is a potential recipient of God's revelation. This stance aligns with the psalmist's assertion, "The secret of the Lord is with them that fear him; and he will show them his covenant" (Ps. 25:14). Thus, Guerra bridges the gap between scholarly theological reflections and lay spiritual experiences.

Furthermore, Guerra's role extends to cultivating a renewed eschatological awareness within the modern Church. Her persistent calls to embrace the Holy Spirit nurture a heightened anticipation of God's final revelation—what theologians term the 'eschaton'. This eschatological vision encapsulates a hope-filled reality where divine truth progressively unfolds, ushering believers towards a consummate understanding of God and His salvific plan. This resonates profoundly with John's apocalyptic vision: "He that hath an ear, let him hear what the Spirit saith unto the churches" (Rev. 3:22).

In conclusion, Blessed Elena Guerra emerges as a pivotal figure in the modern understanding of revelation. Her teachings invigorate the Church to rediscover the kinetic presence of the Holy Spirit, urging a transformative spirituality that finds its roots in the scriptural and apostolic tradition yet speaks compellingly to contemporary faith contexts. Guerra's legacy is a testimony to the ever-present, ever-active revelation of God through the Holy Spirit, offering a perennial invitation to encounter the Divine more intimately and authentically.

Chapter 9: Pentecost and Modern Revelation

Pentecost, as chronicled in the Acts of the Apostles, marks the day when the Holy Spirit descended upon the Apostles, imbuing them with divine power and initiating the missionary work of the early Church. "And there appeared unto them cloven tongues like as of fire, and it sat upon each of them" (Acts 2:3). This vivid imagery underscores a transformative moment, signifying not only the birth of the Church but also the dynamism of divine revelation.

The Pentecost event is not merely an historical phenomenon; it possesses a perennial quality that speaks into the fabric of modern faith. Blessed Elena Guerra, known for her fervent advocacy of Pentecostal spirituality, saw in Pentecost an inexhaustible wellspring of grace, crucial for understanding and experiencing modern revelation. Her teachings emphasize a continuous, unbroken line of divine disclosure that did not cease with the closing of the biblical canon but rather evolves and adapts, inviting humanity into a deeper communion with God.

Guerra's role in modern Catholicism can be understood as a catalyst, urging the Church to embrace a renewed Pentecostal fervor. Her encouragement to Pope Leo XIII led to the promulgation of the encyclical *Divinum Illud Munus* in 1897, highlighting the Holy Spirit's enduring presence and action in the Church. Guerra's work invites us to reflect on how revelation, initiated at Pentecost, continues to unfold in our times through the workings of the Holy Spirit.

The Pentecostal spirit, as advocated by Guerra, establishes a link between the miraculous experiences of the early Church and the existential challenges of the contemporary world. Just as the Apostles were empowered to speak in diverse tongues, today's believers are called to discern the varied languages of modernity—be it scientific, philosophical, or cultural—and to recognize within them the whispers of divine truth.

In this context, the teachings of Karl Rahner and Hans Urs von Balthasar provide further insight into the nature of modern revelation. Rahner's concept of the "supernatural existential" posits that human beings are inherently oriented toward God, and that divine revelation is a constant and integral dimension of human existence. This intrinsic orientation suggests that Pentecost is but a signpost of a more profound truth: our lives are perpetually interfused with the divine.

Von Balthasar, on the other hand, speaks to the aesthetical and dramatic dimensions of revelation. Pentecost, in his theology, is a dramatic encounter between God and humanity, transcending mere historical narrative and entering the realm of the absolute beauty of divine love. Balthasar sees the Holy Spirit as the divine artist, sculpting the unfolding revelation within the mystical body of the Church. In this interplay, Pentecost becomes a timeless event, recurrent in the liturgical life of the Church and the personal experience of each believer.

The convergence of Guerra's advocacy with the theological reflections of Rahner and von Balthasar elucidates a profound truth: Pentecost is not a mere relic of ecclesial history but a living reality perpetually renewing the Church. This perspective invites modern theologians and believers to maintain a vigilant openness to the prompts of the Holy Spirit, always discerning the signs of the times in light of divine revelation.

Finally, the historical context of Pentecost reveals a divine pedagogy that is as relevant today as it was two millennia ago. The tongues of fire, the diverse languages, the bold proclamation—these elements signify the universality and inclusiveness of God's revelation. As the world grapples with fragmentation and division, the message of Pentecost calls for unity in the Spirit, a unity that transcends human boundaries and regenerates the community of believers.

Thus, Pentecost and its significance for modern revelation offer a rich tapestry, woven with threads of historical continuity, theological depth, and experiential dynamism. This event, forever enshrined in the heart of Christianity, beckons us to attune our senses to the ongoing, ever-present revelation of God's infinite love and wisdom.

Historical Context of Pentecost

The event of Pentecost, described in the Acts of the Apostles, marks a cornerstone in Christian history. It is here that the Holy Spirit descended upon the apostles, endowing them with the ability to speak in various tongues, a divine enablement that symbolized the universality of the Gospel. As noted in Acts 2:4, "And they were all filled with the Holy Ghost, and began to speak with other tongues, as the Spirit gave them utterance" (Acts 2:4). This seminal moment not only uncovers a pivotal transformation in the lives of the apostles but also sets the stage for understanding modern revelation through a historical lens.

Historically, Pentecost carries both Judaic and Greek connotations, interpolating significant theological meanings. The Jewish feast of Shavuot, commemorating the giving of the Torah at Mount Sinai, aligns with Pentecost, underscoring the continuity of divine revelation from the Old Covenant to the New. This connection emphasizes God's unbroken communication with His people, which, through the Holy Spirit, reaches a heightened form of universality during Pentecost. It is as if the very fabric of divine revelation expands, weaving together a broader inclusion of humanity beyond ethnic and linguistic boundaries.

In the Jewish tradition, Shavuot is a time of covenantal remembrance, a divine bequest upon His chosen people. Pentecost extends this gift, integrating a more inclusive narrative that signals God's revelation to all nations. This phenomenon is amplified by the apostles' newfound ability to communicate across linguistic divides, heralding a new chapter in divine-human interaction. "And how hear we every man in our own tongue, wherein we were born?" (Acts 2:8).

The theological implications of Pentecost are vast and resonant. It signifies a shift from the particular to the universal, a movement that Karl Rahner might describe as an invitation into the Mystery of God that envelops every human experience. Rahner speaks of God's self-communication as ever-present and dynamic, a sentiment that finds its roots in the very fabric of Pentecost.

Moving to patristic perspectives, St. Augustine's elucidation on the Holy Spirit provides a foundational understanding of Pentecost within the broader Christian theological framework. Augustine frequently describes the Holy Spirit as the bond of love between the Father and the Son, a divine essence that operationalizes God's ongoing revelation to humanity. Augustine refers to this divine process as an inexhaustible wellspring of grace, simultaneously binding the community of believers in love and endowing them with the divine presence.

St. Gregory of Nazianzus, another pillar of early Christian thought, offers additional insights into the revelatory dynamics at work in Pentecost. For Gregory, the Holy Spirit represents the fullness of divine wisdom and an active agent in the sanctification of believers. His theology strongly emphasizes the transformative power of the Holy Spirit, a concept that aligns seamlessly with the miraculous occurrences at Pentecost. Gregory's perspectives on divine wisdom and sanctification highlight the dual nature of Pentecostal revelation: both an immediate, miraculous event and an ongoing, sanctifying action within the Church.

Interestingly, the event of Pentecost does not merely commemorate a historical moment but continues to influence contemporary understandings of divine revelation. Hans Urs von Balthasar's theological exegesis further enriches this discussion by focusing on the glory of God as revealed through the Holy Spirit. Balthasar elucidates the aspect of beauty and divine dramatization evident in the Pentecost event, framing it as both participatory and revelatory.

The intricate tapestry of Pentecostal history weaves together various theological strands, including those articulated by modern theologians. St. Gregory of Nazianzus' description of the Holy Spirit as a purifying flame finds a complementary resonance in von Balthasar's emphasis on divine splendor and theatricality. Both perspectives converge to portray Pentecost as a revelatory event that transcends historical confines, continuing to inform and inspire contemporary theological discourse.

The contributions of Blessed Elena Guerra bring yet another layer to this multifaceted understanding. Guerra's emphasis on the renewal of the Holy Spirit and the revival of Pentecostal fervor within the Church underlines the perennial relevance of this historical event. Her teachings have revitalized interest in the dynamic workings of the Holy Spirit, making Pentecostal theology a vital component of modern revelation.

Through these various theological lenses, it becomes clear that the historical context of Pentecost is far from being a static narrative. It is a dynamic, multi-layered event that serves as a cornerstone for understanding God's continual self-revelation. In both ancient and modern contexts, Pentecost functions as a divine clarion call, inviting humanity into a deeper relationship with the Divine.

Pentecost encapsulates the dialectical nature of revelation – a singular historical event that reverberates through time, impacting individual lives and collective ecclesial consciousness. This intricate tapestry of divine-human interaction presents Pentecost not merely as a relic of the past but as a vivid, pressing reality that captures the ongoing dialectic between God's immanence and transcendence.

Indeed, the Pentecost event provides a vital archetype for understanding the nature of contemporary revelation. Its historical roots and theological implications present a rich milieu for comprehending how divine grace operates within space and time. In essence, the Pentecostal experience reveals a God who is intimately involved in the fabric of human history, continuously inviting humanity into deeper communion through the work of the Holy Spirit.

In conclusion, the historical context of Pentecost serves as a profound elucidation of the universal and dynamic nature of God's revelation. It traces the thread of divine communication from the particularistic covenantal promises of the Old Testament to the universal outpouring of the Holy Spirit upon all flesh. As we move forward in exploring the intersections of modern revelation, the insights gleaned from Pentecost will invariably serve as a foundational touchstone, illuminating the pathways through which God continues to reveal Himself in our contemporary world.

Guerra's Influence and Teachings

Blessed Elena Guerra's influence on the contemporary understanding of Pentecost and modern revelation stands as a beacon of spiritual renewal and ecclesial reform. Her journey began in the late 19th and early 20th centuries, a time marked by significant changes and challenges within the Roman Catholic Church. Guerra's profound devotion to the Holy Spirit and her fervent advocacy for a renewed appreciation of Pentecost emerged as a pivotal movement within the Church, encouraging believers to seek a deeper and more dynamic relationship with the divine.

Guerra's teachings are rooted in a desire to reignite the fervor of the early Church, mirroring the days of the Apostles when the Holy Spirit descended upon them, transforming ordinary individuals into bold proclaimers of the Gospel. Her focus on the Holy Spirit as the catalyst for spiritual renewal speaks to the heart of Christian experience, asserting that it is through the Spirit that God's will and wisdom are revealed to humankind. The words of Christ, "But the Comforter, which is the Holy Ghost, whom the Father will send in my name, he shall teach you all things, and bring all things to your remembrance, whatsoever I have said unto you" (John 14:26), resonate profoundly with Guerra's vision. She emphasized that the Holy Spirit continues to guide and instruct the faithful, making divine mysteries accessible in an ever-changing world.

One of Guerra's most significant contributions was her tireless effort to inspire a more profound devotion to the Holy Spirit through her writings and initiatives. She founded the Oblates of the Holy Spirit, a congregation dedicated to fostering spiritual growth and renewal in the Church. Guerra believed that just as the descent of the Holy Spirit at Pentecost marked the birth of the Church, so too could a renewed outpouring of the Spirit bring about a renaissance in contemporary Christian life. Her emphasis on prayer, particularly the devotion to the Holy Spirit, served as a means of inviting divine intervention and enlightenment.

In her correspondences with Pope Leo XIII, Guerra passionately advocated for a greater emphasis on the Holy Spirit within the Church's liturgy and devotional practices. Her letters were instrumental in leading to the Pope's apostolic letter "Divinum illud munus," which highlighted the essential role of the Holy Spirit in the Church. Guerra's influence was pivotal in ensuring that the Spirit's work was not relegated to a mere theological concept but was recognized as a living and active presence in the lives of believers.

Guerra's teachings also carried a prophetic dimension, urging the Church to be attentive to the signs of the times and to respond with spirit-filled boldness. She perceived modernity not as a threat but as an opportunity for the Church to witness to the transformative power of the Spirit. Her insights echoed the exhortation of the Apostle Paul, "Now the Lord is that Spirit: and where the Spirit of the Lord is, there is liberty" (2 Cor. 3:17). This liberty, according to Guerra, was the freedom to move beyond rigid structures and to embrace a more dynamic expression of faith.

Elena Guerra's legacy is also evident in the way her teachings have permeated various movements within the Catholic Church. The Charismatic Renewal, which emerged in the mid-20th century, echoes Guerra's emphasis on the active presence and gifts of the Holy Spirit. The Renewal sought to revive the charismatic gifts described in the New Testament, such as prophecy, healing, and speaking in tongues, bringing a renewed vibrancy to Catholic spirituality. Guerra's spiritual DNA is discernible in these movements, as they pursue a deeper experiential knowledge of God through the workings of the Holy Spirit.

Furthermore, Guerra's influence extends beyond devotional practices to encompass theological reflections on the nature of revelation. In her view, the Holy Spirit serves as the principal mediator of divine revelation in the present age. This perspective aligns with the broader theological discourse that posits the Spirit as the ongoing agent of God's self-disclosure. Through the Spirit, the mysteries of faith continue to unfold, resonating with the prophetic words found in the Book of Joel, "And it shall come to pass afterward, that I will pour out my spirit upon all flesh; and your sons and your daughters shall prophesy, your old men shall dream dreams, your young men shall see visions" (Joel 2:28).

In the context of modern revelation, Guerra's teachings underscore the continuity and dynamism of God's self-revelation. She argued that the revelation did not cease with the close of the biblical canon but continues through the Spirit's action in the Church and the world. This view challenges the notion of static revelation and invites believers to remain open to the Spirit's guidance in discerning the signs of the times and responding to the needs of the contemporary world.

Guerra's profound impact also lies in her visionary approach to ecumenism and interfaith dialogue. She believed that the Holy Spirit's work transcends denominational boundaries, fostering unity among Christians and promoting mutual understanding among different faith traditions. Her perspective resonates with the Pauline vision of the body of Christ, where diverse gifts and expressions of faith are harmonized by the Spirit, as articulated in 1 Corinthians 12:13, "For by one Spirit are we all baptized into one body, whether we be Jews or Gentiles, whether we be bond or free; and have been all made to drink into one Spirit."

Elena Guerra's influence on modern revelation is also evident in the way she bridged the gap between personal piety and social action. She taught that an authentic encounter with the Holy Spirit should lead to a transformative impact on society, inspiring believers to work for justice, peace, and the common good. Guerra's emphasis on the inseparability of spiritual renewal and social responsibility reflects the integral nature of Christian discipleship, reminiscent of James' exhortation, "Even so faith, if it hath not works, is dead, being alone" (James 2:17).

In synthesizing her teachings, it becomes clear that Guerra's influence extends far beyond her immediate context, offering valuable insights for the Church's engagement with the modern world. Her vision for a Spirit-filled Church that is both deeply rooted in tradition and dynamically responsive to contemporary challenges provides a compelling framework for understanding modern revelation. Her contributions underscore the enduring relevance of the Holy Spirit in guiding the Church towards a fuller realization of God's kingdom on earth.

As we contemplate Guerra's legacy, it is evident that her prophetic voice continues to resonate, calling the Church to a renewed encounter with the Holy Spirit. Her teachings offer a path towards a more vibrant and engaged faith, one that embraces the transformative power of divine revelation in the here and now. Through her influence, we are reminded of the timeless promise of Pentecost and the ever-present work of the Spirit in leading humanity into the fullness of divine truth and love.

Chapter 10: Integrating Historical and Modern Perspectives

The journey through the vast corridors of theological thought, starting with Augustine and Gregory and traversing the complex minds of Rahner, von Balthasar, and Guerra, brings us to a pivotal intersection. Here, history and modernity meet, not as adversaries, but as dance partners in the grand ballet of divine revelation. This chapter endeavors to integrate these rich, varied perspectives into a coherent understanding, unraveling how historical insights illuminate contemporary theology while modern revelations provide new lenses to appreciate ancient wisdom.

Saint Augustine's reflections form a foundational bedrock. His ruminations on the Trinity and divine revelation emphasize the internal process of understanding divine mystery in human language. "Great is our Lord, and of great power: his understanding is infinite" (Psalm 147:5). Augustine's conception of the Trinity as a mirror of the human experience—mind, knowledge, and love—remains profoundly relevant. His insights into the relational nature of God underscore a timeless truth: that revelation is not merely informational but transformational.

As Augustine articulates the internal dynamism of the Trinity, Gregory of Nazianzus offers a complementary vision. His poetics and precision, particularly his sermons and theological orations, beckon us to consider the relational dynamics within the Godhead. Gregory's emphasis on the experiential encounter with God reminds us that revelation is deeply personal. Theophany, or divine appearance, as experienced in the lives of saints and mystics, is Gregory's testament to a God who is intimately involved in creation—"For with thee is the fountain of life: in thy light shall we see light" (Psalm 36:9).

In synthesizing these patristic perspectives, Karl Rahner emerges with an insistence on the immediacy of divine revelation in the modern world. Rahner contended that God's self-communication is intrinsic to human experience. His concept of the "supernatural existential" situates divine grace not as an abstract addition to human nature but intrinsic to it. The divine mystery is always already present, beckoning humanity to recognize and respond—"In him we live, and move, and have our being" (Acts 17:28).

This notion is complemented by Hans Urs von Balthasar, who unfurls the aesthetic dimension of theology. Balthasar's emphasis on beauty as a transcendental that reveals God introduces an incarnational dynamic to revelation. He suggests that the glory of God is manifest in the splendor of creation and that this beauty directs us to the ultimate expression of divine revelation in the person of Jesus Christ. "The heavens declare

the glory of God; and the firmament sheweth his handywork"
(Psalm 19:1).

Further enriching this tapestry is Blessed Elena Guerra, whose
fervent advocacy for a renewed appreciation of the Holy Spirit
during Pentecost brings a charismatic vitality to theological
discourse. Guerra's focus on the living presence of the Spirit
highlights the continuity of revelation from the early church to
contemporary times. The Spirit, as the agent of Pentecost,
actively participates in the unfolding of history, impelling the
church to new expressions of faith and understanding—"But ye
shall receive power, after that the Holy Ghost is come upon you"
(Acts 1:8).

The interplay between these historical and modern voices does
not suggest a mere chronological succession but rather a rich,
interwoven tapestry. Augustine's internal dynamism, Gregory's
experiential encounters, Rahner's immediacy of divine presence,
Balthasar's aesthetic theology, and Guerra's Pentecostal
fervor—each contributes a vital thread. Together, they provide a
unified understanding of modern revelation. This holistic view
acknowledges that revelation is both a historical continuum and
dynamically new, addressing the evolving context of human
existence.

Integrating these perspectives necessitates recognizing the intrinsic coherence in the divine economy. The Holy Spirit, as the animator of both historical and modern thought, ensures that the insights of the past are not relics but living wisdom. This is exemplified in the continuity of Trinitarian theology from Augustine and Gregory through Rahner and von Balthasar to contemporary reflections inspired by Guerra. The Trinitarian God, revealed as Father, Son, and Holy Spirit, remains the central mystery, inviting deeper contemplation and more profound understanding.

Furthermore, this synthesis invites us to revisit the nature of ecclesial tradition. Tradition is not static but dynamic, encompassing the living faith of the church. Rahner's concept of the "anonymous Christian," who experiences God's grace unknowingly, and Balthasar's idea of the "dramatic" nature of revelation, where human history becomes the stage for divine self-disclosure, challenge us to expand our theological horizons. They call for an ecclesiology that is open, dialogical, and attentive to the signs of the times—"Therefore be ye also ready: for in such an hour as ye think not the Son of man cometh" (Matt. 24:44).

In this integration, the role of the theologian emerges as critical. Theologians must navigate the tension between preserving the integrity of historical insights and engaging with contemporary questions and challenges. This task requires a hermeneutic rooted in fidelity, creativity, and discernment. It demands a faith that is as rigorous as it is open, as mystical as it is rational. The theologian becomes a bridge, linking the wisdom of the ages with the fresh insights of the present, always attentive to the Spirit's guidance—"For the Spirit searcheth all things, yea, the deep things of God" (1 Cor. 2:10).

No less critical is the role of the community of believers. Revelation is not a solitary enterprise but a communal journey. The church, as the body of Christ, participates in this ongoing unveiling of divine mystery. The liturgy, sacraments, prayer, and acts of charity—all become loci where revelation occurs. This communal aspect underscores that understanding divine revelation is not solely the task of scholars but of the entire people of God. Together, they are called to discern, celebrate, and embody the ongoing self-disclosure of God—"Where two or three are gathered together in my name, there am I in the midst of them" (Matt. 18:20).

The synthesis of historical and modern perspectives illuminates that divine revelation is a symphony—complex, multilayered, and harmonious. It resonates with ancient themes even as it introduces new movements, guided by the Spirit, who "bloweth where it listeth" (John 3:8). Through this integration, we gain a deeper appreciation for the richness of God's self-communication, capable of speaking to every age, every culture, every heart.

Thus, as we draw from the deep wells of Augustine's introspective theology, Gregory's pastoral wisdom, Rahner's existential perspective, Balthasar's aesthetic vision, and Guerra's charismatic fervor, we find a unified yet multifaceted understanding of modern revelation. This chapter underscores that the God who reveals is not confined by time but engages with history dynamically, fostering a living tradition that speaks anew to each generation. "Jesus Christ the same yesterday, and today,

Synthesizing the Views of Augustine, Gregory, Rahner, von Balthasar, and Guerra

To comprehend modern revelation in its fullness, it is essential to weave together the threads spun by Augustine, Gregory, Rahner, von Balthasar, and Guerra. Their theological insights collectively enrich the tapestry of contemporary understanding, creating a symphony of perspectives that resonate through time.

Augustine's conception of the Trinity forms the cornerstone of Christian revelation. His profound meditations on the nature of God—Father, Son, and Holy Spirit—echo through his writings and provide a foundational framework. Augustine's interpretation emphasizes the inner life of the Trinity, highlighting the relational aspect of God's revelation to humanity. "He that loveth not knoweth not God; for God is love" (1 John 4:8) encapsulates Augustine's vision, wherein revelation is an enduring encounter with divine love.

Meanwhile, Gregory of Nazianzus contributes a dynamic and intricate perspective on the Trinity, accentuating the coexistence and coeternity of the three Persons. His reflections are not merely theological abstractions but are deeply pastoral and spiritual. Gregory sees the revelation in terms of a transformative experience, where the believer is drawn into the divine mystery. His thoughts align well with the scriptural assertion, "For now we see through a glass, darkly; but then face to face" (1 Cor. 13:12), which speaks to the progressive unfolding of God's self-disclosure.

Rahner's transcendental theology introduces a modern lens through which divine revelation can be perceived. His idea that God communicates through the depth of human consciousness is revolutionary. Rahner posits that every human experience of mystery and transcendence is a potential encounter with God's revelation. He affirms, "For in him we live, and move, and have our being" (Acts 17:28), urging an integration of the divine with the human experience.

Von Balthasar offers a complementary but distinct vision. His theology revolves around the dramatic character of revelation, where God reveals Himself in history through a series of divine acts, culminating in the person of Jesus Christ. Von Balthasar underscores the aesthetic dimension of revelation—how beauty, truth, and goodness converge to manifest God's love. "And the Word was made flesh, and dwelt among us" (John 1:14) reflects his emphasis on the incarnation as the apex of divine self-revelation.

In contrast, but no less important, Blessed Elena Guerra's charism centers on Pentecost and the work of the Holy Spirit. Guerra's teachings invite a renewed focus on the Spirit's ongoing revelatory activity in the Church and the world. She champions a spirituality that seeks the Spirit's guidance in contemporary contexts, reminding believers that "the Spirit itself beareth witness with our spirit, that we are the children of God" (Rom. 8:16). Her influence underscores the continuous nature of divine revelation, as the Spirit breathes life and insight into the modern Church.

Each theologian, through their unique approach, contributes a vital piece to the puzzle of understanding God's revelation today. Augustine and Gregory lay the foundational bedrock with their Trinitarian theology. Rahner and von Balthasar expand this foundation into the realms of human experience and historical drama. Guerra bridges this continuum by emphasizing the active and vibrant presence of the Holy Spirit.

By synthesizing these views, we observe a multifaceted portrait of revelation that both respects tradition and embraces modernity. Their collective wisdom urges the faithful to recognize that revelation is not a static, one-time event but an ongoing, dynamic relationship between God and humanity. Theologians and philosophers can find in their teachings a robust framework for exploring the depths of divine mystery, while scientists might appreciate the nuanced way these insights affirm a universe imbued with meaning and purpose.

Augustine's contemplative approach teaches us to seek God in the depths of our hearts. Gregory's theological symmetry invites us to contemplate the complexity and unity of divine life. Rahner's transcendental method encourages us to perceive divine whispers in our everyday experiences. Von Balthasar's dramatic focus urges us to engage with revelation as an unfolding narrative that illuminates history. Finally, Guerra calls us to attune ourselves to the Spirit's ongoing revelations, reminding us that God continues to speak into the heart of the Church and the world.

Thus, the integration of these perspectives creates a rich theological mosaic. Augustine and Gregory's Trinitarian insights provide the doctrinal scaffolding upon which the dynamic processes described by Rahner, von Balthasar, and Guerra can be understood and appreciated. This synthesis demonstrates that the revelation is an inherently relational, historical, and spiritual phenomenon, characterized by a perpetual interplay between the human and the divine.

The unified understanding of revelation that arises from this synthesis is an invitation to see the divine in all aspects of life. It calls us to marvel at the mystery of the Trinity, engage with the tangible reality of Christ's incarnation, and remain open to the Spirit's transformative work. This comprehensive vision urges a pastoral application that is as much about guiding believers into the divine mystery as it is about affirming the richness of Christian tradition within a modern context.

In practical terms, this synthesis can profoundly impact worship, devotion, and evangelization. It advocates for a holistic approach that incorporates the wisdom of the Church Fathers with the insights of contemporary theologians, creating a robust foundation for a living faith. By embracing this integrated approach, the contemporary Church can navigate the complexities of the modern world while remaining anchored in the timeless truths of divine revelation.

In summary, the converging views of Augustine, Gregory, Rahner, von Balthasar, and Guerra provide a multifaceted and coherent understanding of modern revelation. Their combined insights reveal a God who is both transcendent and immanent, unchanging and dynamic, personal and communal. This synthesis not only deepens our theological understanding but also enriches our spiritual lives, inviting us to encounter a God who perpetually reveals Himself in love, beauty, and truth.

The Unified Understanding of Modern Revelation

The unified understanding of modern revelation necessitates a confluence of historical theology and contemporary thought, seamlessly integrating the paradigms of Augustine, Gregory, Rahner, von Balthasar, and Guerra. This chapter, then, does not merely reiterate the individual contributions of these theological giants but weaves them into a cohesive tapestry reflecting the divine's ever-unfolding self-disclosure. The notion of revelation is neither static nor confined to past epochs; it is a living encounter, resonating with the ecclesial and existential realities of believers today.

St. Augustine, with his profound Trinitarian insights, lays the groundwork for understanding revelation as a relational act of God. He perceives divine revelation not as a mere dispensation of doctrines but as an invitation into the life of the Trinity. "For there are three that bear record in heaven, the Father, the Word, and the Holy Ghost: and these three are one" (1 John 5:7). Augustine's emphasis on the love that binds the Trinity offers a glimpse into the loving nature of revelation itself—a self-giving and relational act. This relational aspect finds echoes in modern theological explorations, where revelation is seen as God's self-communication in love.

Turning to Gregory of Nazianzus, his theological contributions further illuminate the Trinitarian dynamics of revelation. Gregory's insights into the distinct yet unified roles of the Father, Son, and Holy Spirit accentuate how revelation unfolds in a pluriform yet cohesive manner. "The grace of the Lord Jesus Christ, and the love of God, and the communion of the Holy Ghost, be with you all. Amen" (2 Cor. 13:14). Herein, Gregory's articulation of the divine economy serves as a lens through which modern theology can view revelation: multifaceted yet integrally one.

Karl Rahner's theology advances this understanding by positing that revelation is God's self-communication occurring within the realm of human experience. Rahner's insistence that God can be encountered in the profundity of everyday life transforms the understanding of revelation from a distant, nearly inaccessible event to an immediate, personal experience. This personalization of divine revelation finds further enrichment in Rahner's inclusive theology, which recognizes God's self-disclosure across various cultures and epochs.

Similarly, von Balthasar's focus on the drama of divine revelation expands this horizon, portraying it as an unfolding narrative in which humanity participates. In this divine drama, Christ stands at the center, the pivotal point of revelation. "And the Word was made flesh, and dwelt among us" (John 1:14).

Balthasar's imaginative and aesthetic approach to theology facilitates a deeper appreciation of how revelation engages the senses and the imagination, making the divine palpable in the human story.

Complementing these theological perspectives, Blessed Elena Guerra's teachings introduce a pneumatological dimension, emphasizing the role of the Holy Spirit in modern revelation. Guerra's focus on Pentecost and the charisms highlights the continued vivacity of divine revelation, not merely as a historical event but as an ongoing process ignited by the Holy Spirit. "And when the day of Pentecost was fully come, they were all with one accord in one place. And they were all filled with the Holy Ghost, and began to speak with other tongues" (Acts 2:1, 4). Guerra underscores that the Spirit's work is not confined to the nascent Church but extends dynamically into the present day, further enriching the notion of revelation.

This synthesis calls for a reevaluation of how revelation functions within the life of the Church and individual believers. It is not a static deposit of divine truths but an ongoing, dynamic encounter that perpetually calls the faithful deeper into the mystery of God. These various theological perspectives propose that revelation is, at its core, an invitation into deeper communion with the divine, facilitated by the interplay of the Father, Son, and Holy Spirit.

Moreover, understanding modern revelation necessitates an openness to the dialogical nature of God's self-disclosure. Augustine's relational framework, Gregory's Trinitarian articulation, Rahner's experiential focus, Balthasar's dramaturgical approach, and Guerra's pneumatological emphasis collectively point toward a God who reveals Himself in relationship, narrative, and Spirit-filled action. This dialogical dimension compels believers to recognize revelation as a call to respond, to engage in a transformative dialogue with the divine. "He that hath ears to hear, let him hear" (Matt. 11:15).

Ultimately, the unified understanding of modern revelation is deeply rooted in the interrelation of historical and contemporary perspectives. The faith of the early Church, encapsulated in the teachings of Augustine and Gregory, finds its contemporary expression through the theologies of Rahner, von Balthasar, and the charismatic renewal advocated by Guerra. Together, they reveal a God who is continuously speaking, inviting, and engaging with humanity in ways that are both timeless and timely.

This symphony of theological voices offers a holistic view of revelation that is richly textured and multidimensional. It challenges the Church to recognize that revelation is not merely about divine dictation but about divine dialogue—a profound sharing rooted in eternal truth and adapted to contemporary contexts. "In the beginning was the Word, and the Word was with God, and the Word was God" (John 1:1). Through this integrated approach, the faithful are drawn into the living Word, constantly encountering God's loving self-revelation.

Thus, the unified understanding of modern revelation is not an endpoint but a beginning, an invitation to journey deeper into the mystery of divine love and truth. It demands a continual openness to the Spirit's movement and a readiness to encounter God in the humility of human experience and the grandeur of divine mystery. This integrative approach unites the wisdom of the past with the insights of the present, offering a path forward for engaging with the infinite depth of God's self-revelation. With hearts attuned to the Spirit, believers can enter ever more profoundly into the fullness of divine life and love, embracing a revelation that is both ancient and ever-new.

Chapter 11: Revelation in the Context of Faith and Reason

As we delve into Revelation, we confront the age-old dialectic of faith and reason, a tension and harmony that has occupied the minds of theologians, philosophers, and scientists alike. Both realms offer windows into understanding the divine, yet they often do so in seemingly contradictory ways.

Faith is the assurance of things hoped for, the conviction of things not seen (Heb. 11:1). It transcends empirical evidence, drawing believers into a relationship with God through unseen, yet deeply felt, truths. Reason, on the other hand, demands evidence, arguments, and rational explanations. This juxtaposition is not a battle; rather, it is a dance between ways of knowing, compelling a deeper exploration into the heart of divine revelation.

For Saint Augustine, the interplay between faith and reason was crucial. He argued that faith precedes understanding: "I believe in order to understand" (credo ut intelligam). Augustine held that reason could illuminate faith, offering intellectual coherence to spiritual truths. In his view, revelation was not solely mystical but also profoundly rational, inviting the believer to a fuller intellectual encounter with God.

Moving forward to a more modern context, Karl Rahner's theological perspectives offer a profound synthesis where faith and reason coalesce. Rahner posits that God's revelation permeates through the existential experiences of human life. It is both transcendent and immanent, making use of reason to comprehend the mysteries unveiled by faith. "God is ever greater," Rahner points out, suggesting that divine mystery always surpasses human understanding, yet it is also ever nearer, accessible through the internal dialogue of faith and rational inquiry.

Similarly, Hans Urs von Balthasar's theology places a significant emphasis on aesthetics and beauty, which he sees as an avenue through which divine revelation penetrates human comprehension. For von Balthasar, beauty becomes a bridge facilitating the merger of faith and reason. The splendor of truth is thus perceived not merely through logical constructs but also through the beauty that points us towards the divine, turning our gaze from the earthly to the eternal. This perspective aligns with the Psalmist: "The heavens declare the glory of God; and the firmament sheweth his handywork" (Ps. 19:1).

In contrast to the theologians, scientific perspectives on revelation often ground themselves in natural theology—the belief that knowledge of God can be acquired through reason and the observation of nature. This view echoes Romans: "For the invisible things of him from the creation of the world are clearly seen, being understood by the things that are made"

(Rom. 1:20). Natural theology does not oppose divine revelation but seeks to understand it through the lens of rational inquiry into the natural world.

One philosopher who bridged faith and reason ingeniously is Thomas Aquinas. While not a central figure in this book, his influence cannot be overstated. Aquinas argued that faith and reason are harmonious, with both aiming toward the same truth. Reason, for Aquinas, delineated the natural truths about God, while faith illuminated the supernatural truths that lie beyond human reason's grasp. His famous Five Ways, or proofs for the existence of God, are a testament to his belief in the complementarity of faith and rational inquiry.

The scientific revolution presented a formidable challenge to this harmony, yet it also offered fresh avenues for integrating faith and reason. Scientists like Galileo and Newton, despite their complex relationships with the church, sought to understand the cosmos in ways that acknowledged a divine creator. Today, discussions in cosmology, quantum mechanics, and biology continue to enrich theological reflections on revelation.

Quantum mechanics, in particular, has reopened discussions about the nature of reality and the limits of human knowledge, paralleling theological inquiries into the mystery and majesty of

God's actions. For example, the indeterminacy inherent in quantum theory challenges classical notions of causality and encourages a humility before the mysteries of both the cosmos and God's interaction with creation.

In this context, the works of contemporary theologians like Karl Rahner and Hans Urs von Balthasar serve as vital resources. Rahner's concept of the "supernatural existential," which proposes that every person is inherently ordered toward the divine by virtue of their existence, offers a powerful framework for understanding revelation as an ever-present reality. Von Balthasar's focus on beauty as a manifestation of divine truth complements this by emphasizing that revelation can be encountered through the senses as well as through intellectual contemplation.

Faith and reason, when drawn together, form a more comprehensive view of revelation. The Catholic intellectual tradition has never shied away from this synthesis. As articulated in the First Vatican Council's *Dei Filius*, and reaffirmed in the Second Vatican Council's *Dei Verbum*, the Church maintains that there can be no true discord between faith and reason because they both derive from the same divine source.

Consider the example of the Incarnation, which stands at the heart of Christian faith. The Word becoming flesh (John 1:14) defies purely rational explanation, yet it invites the faithful to understand the divine through reason. The objective truth of Christ's divinity and humanity is a revelation that plunges one into the mysteries of faith, while also compelling rational exploration of its implications for humanity and the cosmos.

In contemporary dialogue, theologians and scientists often engage in discussions at the intersection of faith and reason. These conversations underscore the necessity of maintaining a delicate balance, ensuring that neither domain silences the other. The magisterium of the Church continues to encourage such dialogue, reflecting the belief that truth is one, whether found through the microscope, the telescope, or the contemplative prayer.

Concluding, the harmony between faith and reason in the context of revelation reveals a profound unity in the quest for truth. As both Augustine and Aquinas taught, and as Rahner and von Balthasar exemplified in their works, the pursuit of understanding—whether through philosophical reasoning or theological contemplation—leads ultimately to the divine. Faith and reason are not adversaries but companions on the journey toward the fullness of truth manifested in God's revelation.

Philosophical Underpinnings

The intersection of faith and reason, especially within the context of revelation, invokes a rich philosophical tradition that seeks to understand the very nature of how the divine communicates with humanity. This sacred dialogue between the Eternal and the temporal has been considered through various lenses—metaphysical, epistemological, and existential. Our journey through the philosophical underpinnings of revelation must pay homage to the contributions of Augustine, Gregory, Rahner, von Balthasar, and Guerra, whose perspectives illuminate the path toward a comprehensive understanding of divine communication.

Augustine of Hippo, in his introspective quest for truth, rooted his understanding of revelation in a profound integration of Platonic thought and Christian theology. For Augustine, the finite human intellect can grasp divine truths only through the illumination by the divine light, a notion resembling Plato's Theory of Forms but reinterpreted in a Christian paradigm. "For with thee is the fountain of life: in thy light shall we see light" (Ps. 36:9), Augustine would frequently refer to such verses to emphasize how God's illumination allows humans to apprehend higher truths.

Gregory of Nazianzus, meanwhile, calls for a contemplative approach, recognizing the limits of human reason while also affirming the necessity of divine grace. His apophatic theology, expressing God as beyond human comprehension, stresses the importance of mystical knowledge over purely rational explanations. This emphasis reverberates through his homilies and hymns, wherein Gregory often juxtaposes human ignorance with divine omniscience, effectively advocating for humility and reverence in theological exploration.

Against this backdrop, Karl Rahner's transcendental theology presents a more modern approach, weaving existential philosophy into the fabric of Christian revelation. Rahner proposes that every person has a latent awareness of the divine, a supernatural existential, that predisposes them to receive revelation. This potentiality is actualized in the concrete historical event of God's self-communication through Jesus Christ. In Rahner's visionary articulation, revelation is not confined to static doctrinal propositions but is a dynamic encounter that calls for an existential response from the individual.

Hans Urs von Balthasar complements Rahner by emphasizing the aesthetic dimension of revelation, where beauty serves as a pathway to truth. Drawing from a rich tapestry of literary and artistic traditions, von Balthasar asserts that the divine glory is evident in worldly beauty, leading the soul to a fuller comprehension of God. His theologically nuanced aesthetical approach prominently places Christ's incarnation as the ultimate revelation, revealing the divine in the most tangible sense. Balthasar's use of dramatic analogy offers a profound narrative that engages both the intellect and the imagination.

Elena Guerra, though less quoted in philosophical discourses, brings an essential element to our understanding through her focus on the Holy Spirit and Pentecost. Her insights reflect a pneumatological dimension where the Spirit transcends human understanding and yet immanently communicates God's will and love. Guerra's teachings remind us that Revelation is not solely an epistemic venture but is fundamentally relational, inviting believers to experience and embody God's love in communal worship and individual devotion.

Thus, a unified philosophical undercurrent flows through the thoughts of our theologians: revelation is both an epistemic and existential encounter, bridging the finite and the Infinite. To comprehend divine revelation within the context of faith and reason, one must balance these dimensions, cognizant of human limitations while open to divine transcendence.

The cumulative wisdom from Augustine to Guerra underscores that reason and faith are not adversaries but companions on the journey to understanding revelation. Rather than presenting faith as blind trust or reason as sterile logic, they advocate for a harmonious relationship where reason illuminates faith and faith deepens reason. As "the Spirit itself beareth witness with our spirit, that we are the children of God" (Rom. 8:16), this mutual witness underscores the complementary roles of faith and reason in comprehending divine truth.

The philosophical bedrock discussed here lays a foundation that resists reductionism and embraces complexity. Augustine's illumination theory, Gregory's mystical reverence, Rahner's existential horizon, von Balthasar's aesthetic contemplation, and Guerra's pneumatological emphasis collectively offer a multidimensional framework. These perspectives, when interwoven, guide us toward a richer, fuller understanding of revelation that speaks to both the heart and the mind, echoing eternal truths in temporal experience.

In understanding revelation's philosophical underpinnings, we are led to see that divine truths are participatory, inviting us into a dynamic experience rather than a mere intellectual assent. This participatory nature mandates an engagement not only with sacred texts and traditions but also with the experiential realities of prayer, worship, and community life, reinforcing the idea that revelation is lived as much as it's understood.

As we navigate the complex terrain of faith and reason, the insights offered by these theological giants compel us to engage deeply with both scripture and tradition. The Biblical witness, like the one provided in Romans 1:20, "For the invisible things of him from the creation of the world are clearly seen, being understood by the things that are made," encourages us to discern God's hand in the world around us, blending the natural and the supernatural in our pursuit of knowledge.

In summary, the philosophical underpinnings of revelation in the context of faith and reason form a robust and dynamic framework that stretches from Augustine's metaphysical illumination to Guerra's Spirit-led piety. Through this multifaceted lens, we see divine revelation as a continuous, living dialogue that invites us into a deeper communion with the Divine, forever probing, and being probed by, the mystery of God's self-disclosure.

Scientific Perspectives

In our quest to explore revelation within the framework of faith and reason, we must traverse the uncharted waters where theology intersects with scientific thought. This intersection, often seen as contentious, has been the fertile ground from which modern intellectual giants, both theologians and scientists, have drawn inspiration and insight. The scientific perspectives, particularly from the realms of cosmology, biology, and quantum physics, challenge and enrich our theological understanding of divine revelation.

Cosmology, the study of the origin and development of the universe, invites us to ponder the grandeur and complexity of creation. The Biblical proclamation, "In the beginning God created the heaven and the earth" (Gen. 1:1), takes on new dimensions when viewed through the lens of the Big Bang theory. This scientific narrative of a universe expanding from a singularity echoes the theological concept of creatio ex nihilo, creation out of nothing. The astonishing precision with which the fundamental constants of the universe are set can be seen as a testament to divine wisdom, suggesting that the cosmos itself is a kind of revelation, a physical testament to the Creator's majesty and intentionality.

Biology, particularly the study of evolution, has famously sparked debate between science and faith. Yet, when viewed through a lens that embraces both the findings of science and the truths of faith, evolution reveals an aspect of God's dynamic creativity. The scripture that declares, "For thou hast possessed my reins: thou hast covered me in my mother's womb. I will praise thee; for I am fearfully and wonderfully made" (Psalm 139:13-14), reminds us that the processes which lead to the diversity of life are part of God's sustaining and ongoing act of creation. Evolution, with its intricate mechanisms and adaptive innovations, speaks to a God who works not in static acts but through a continuous process of elaboration and revelation.

Quantum physics, perhaps the most enigmatic of all sciences, alters our perception of reality itself. Classical mechanics offered a predictable, clockwork universe, but quantum mechanics introduces uncertainty and profundity at the most fundamental levels of matter and energy. This paradigm shift has theological implications, such as in the understanding of divine action in the world. Concepts like wave-particle duality and quantum entanglement suggest a universe far more interconnected and mysterious than previously thought. These notions invite contemplation of how God's omnipresence and omnipotence might be understood in a world where the underlying fabric of reality is so profoundly intertwined and dependent on observation itself.

For theologians like Karl Rahner, the mystery revealed by contemporary science harmonizes with the mystery of divine self-revelation. Rahner posited that human beings are inherently open to the infinite, an openness that modern scientific discoveries can amplify and clarify. Similarly, Hans Urs von Balthasar's emphasis on the aesthetic and dramatic nature of revelation is enriched by the awe-inspiring beauty and complexity of the cosmos as revealed by science. Their theological frameworks, when combined with scientific discoveries, provide a robust paradigm for understanding revelation.

Moreover, St. Augustine's reflections on creation resonate with the unfolding narrative of contemporary cosmology. Augustine's assertion that time itself was a part of creation aligns strikingly with the modern conception of the space-time continuum. His emphasis on God's timelessness contrasts beautifully with the temporality and evolution we observe in the physical universe. By exploring the intersections between Augustine's thought and the scientific narrative, we can appreciate a more profound theological appreciation of creation as an ongoing divine act.

Considering the insights of St. Gregory of Nazianzus, we find that his focus on the impossibility of fully comprehending the divine aligns remarkably well with the mysteries unveiled by quantum mechanics. Gregory's teachings emphasize that human reason is inherently limited when it comes to grasping the fullness of God's essence. The counterintuitive and almost paradoxical nature of quantum physics serves as a metaphor for the transcendence and immanence of God. Just as we struggle to understand particle behavior, we likewise grapple with divine mysteries.

Blessed Elena Guerra's teachings on the Holy Spirit also find resonance within scientific exploration. She emphasized the Spirit's continuing action in the world, which parallels the constant unfolding of natural processes. This ongoing pneumatological activity manifests in the dynamic and evolving cosmos, prompting us to perceive the Holy Spirit like the 'breath' invigorating all creation. Guerra's perspective can encourage us to look at scientific discoveries not as threats to faith but as deeper insights into the workings of the divine Spirit in the world.

In summary, scientific perspectives offer a potent avenue for deepening our understanding of divine revelation. Accepting the insights of cosmology, biology, and quantum physics enables us to view God's self-disclosure in a manner that transcends the dichotomy between science and religion. As science unveils the intricacies of the cosmos, from the vastness of galaxies to the subtle dance of subatomic particles, it provides a fresh canvas upon which the beauty, wisdom, and mystery of God's revelation can be further appreciated.

The harmony between scientific discovery and theological reflection not only enriches our intellectual pursuits but also nourishes our faith. Within this synthesis, we find a robust framework for appreciating modern revelation, one that resonates with Augustine's theological rigor, Rahner's existential depth, von Balthasar's aesthetic vision, Gregory's mystical insight, and Guerra's spirited teachings. By embracing scientific perspectives, we open new horizons for experiencing and understanding the divine, remaining ever mindful that, as St. Paul writes, "For now we see through a glass, darkly; but then face to face" (1 Cor. 13:12).

Chapter 12: Practical Implications of Modern Revelation

Modern revelation has transcended the confines of historical antecedents, shaping the liturgical, intellectual, and evangelical practices of our times. At its core, modern revelation calls for a dynamic engagement with the divine, beckoning us to continually reconfigure our understanding of God's presence in a rapidly evolving world. The implications for worship, devotion, and evangelization are both profound and numerous.

We begin by exploring the impact on worship and devotion. Augustine's assertion that "our hearts are restless until they rest in Thee" unveils the intrinsic human yearning for divine intimacy. This restless heart finds its solace in the communal acts of worship and private moments of devotion. In today's context, this means an integration of traditional liturgies with modern forms of expression, fostering a worship experience that resonates with contemporary sensibilities.

The Eucharistic celebration remains a prime locus for encountering modern revelation. The sacrament of the Eucharist is more than a mere ritual; it is a real, tangible intersection of the human and divine. As we partake in the Eucharist, we are invited to experience Christ's perpetual self-giving—an encounter that is as relevant today as it was at the

Last Supper: "This is my body which is given for you: this do in remembrance of me" (Luke 22:19).

Contemporary worship must also embrace the technological advances at our disposal. The use of multimedia presentations, digital scriptures, and even virtual reality experiences can deepen our engagement with the divine mysteries. By melding ancient practices with modern tools, we create a worship space that is both timeless and timely.

Beyond the sanctuary, devotion in the modern era can take on new forms through daily practices influenced by digital connectivity. Social media platforms and spiritual apps offer daily reflections, prayer reminders, and community support, making it easier for individuals to maintain a steady devotional life despite the busyness of their schedules. Augustine's spiritual method of examining one's conscience and maintaining a rhythm of prayer can now be aided by the very devices that were once deemed distractions.

Moving from personal devotion to communal practice, we see that modern revelation also informs our approach to evangelization. The imperative "Go ye into all the world, and preach the gospel to every creature" (Mark 16:15) remains, but the methods of its fulfillment must adapt to reach diverse audiences. Evangelization today is not solely about preaching from pulpits but involves entering into dialogues facilitated by new media and secular forums.

Hans Urs von Balthasar reminds us of the beauty in the divine revelation that draws people in. Evangelizers must, therefore, present the Gospel in a manner that captures the aesthetic and existential yearnings of the contemporary mind. This entails a storytelling approach that invites encounter rather than confrontation, empathy instead of judgment.

An important aspect of modern evangelization is the concept of "pre-evangelization," a phase where the implicit values of the Gospel are communicated through actions before explicit proclamation. In an age where skepticism towards organized religion is prevalent, embodying the principles of love, justice, and compassion serves as a potent witness to the transformative power of Christ. These pre-evangelizing acts pave the way for deeper discussions about faith and belief.

Furthermore, the integration of faith and reason finds particular relevance in contemporary evangelization. Karl Rahner's notion of the "anonymous Christian" suggests that God's grace can be at work even in those who have not expressly embraced the Christian faith. This insight encourages a dialogical rather than adversarial approach to evangelization, recognizing the work of the Spirit beyond the visible boundaries of the Church.

In educational settings, the teachings of revelation must be inculcated with an awareness of the cultural and intellectual climates of today. Theology should converse with science, philosophy, and the humanities to reveal a holistic understanding of truth. This interdisciplinary approach not only broadens the scope of theological discourse but also renders it more accessible and relatable.

St. Gregory of Nazianzus, with his emphasis on the Trinity, provides a robust framework for understanding relational dynamics. This Trinitarian model underscores the importance of community and interpersonal relationships as reflective of divine communion. Consequently, modern evangelization strategies should promote community-building efforts and foster environments where meaningful relationships can thrive.

Lastly, the influence of Blessed Elena Guerra and her focus on Pentecost reveal the necessity for invoking the Holy Spirit in all our endeavors. The Spirit's guidance ensures that our worship, devotion, and missions are rooted in divine wisdom. "But ye shall receive power, after that the Holy Ghost is come upon you: and ye shall be witnesses unto me" (Acts 1:8) emphasizes the need for divine empowerment in our contemporary context.

In sum, the practical implications of modern revelation call for an inventive and responsive Church. We must infuse our worship with the vitality of both tradition and innovation, transform our personal devotion through contemporary aids, and reimagine evangelization to meet the world as it is. By doing so, we stay true to the essence of the divine message, making it ever new and ever relatable to every generation.

Impact on Worship and Devotion

Modern revelation stands as a beacon, illuminating the landscape of worship and devotion in our contemporary lives. It's not merely an abstract theological concept but a transformative force reshaping our approach to the divine. Historically, revelation provided structured guidance on worship, often rooted in scripture and tradition. However, today, it demands a more dynamic engagement, one that resonates deeply with personal and communal spiritual practices.

When reflecting on modern revelation through the lens of Augustine, we are reminded of the profound intimacy in our relationship with the Triune God. Augustine's compelling imagery of God's indwelling presence invites a more contemplative and personal form of worship. As he eloquently states, "Thou hast made us for Thyself, and our hearts are restless until they find their rest in Thee." This restlessness drives us to seek deeper encounters with God, which modern revelation facilitates by offering fresh insights into divine mysteries.

In the context of communal worship, Karl Rahner's theology enriches our liturgical practices. Rahner emphasizes the omnipresence of grace and God's self-communication as integral to all aspects of life. As such, every moment becomes an opportunity for worship. His perspective encourages the faithful to find sacramental significance in daily activities, thus blurring the lines between sacred and secular. This holistic approach makes the devotion to God an ongoing dialogue rather than a periodic ritual.

For Balthasar, the aesthetic experience plays a vital role in understanding revelation. He describes the encounter with God's beauty as an act of worship in itself. Thus, the liturgical space becomes more than a venue for rituals; it's a theater of divine beauty. The rich symbolism, art, and music employed in worship aim to elevate the soul, urging the faithful to participate in the divine drama. This becomes especially pertinent in contemporary settings where aesthetic and emotive experiences can deepen one's devotional life.

The teachings of Gregory of Nazianzus add another layer to our understanding. Gregory emphasizes the mystery of the Trinity, which invites worshippers into a profound reverence and awe. The complexity and unity of the Trinitarian relationship prompt a more reflective and meditative form of worship. This reflection manifests in prolonged prayer and silence, allowing space for the 'still small voice' of God to speak. As Scripture reminds us, "Be still, and know that I am God" (Ps. 46:10).

Blessed Elena Guerra's influence on devotion cannot be overlooked. Her emphasis on the Holy Spirit and the necessity of Pentecost reveals a vivid picture of active and dynamic worship. For Guerra, modern revelation through the Spirit calls for an enlivened, charismatic devotion that goes beyond mere formality. Her teachings advocate for a fervent spirituality marked by expectant prayer, communal discernment, and active witnessing.

In synthesizing these perspectives, we see that modern revelation offers a multi-dimensional impact on worship and devotion. It encourages personal introspection and communal celebration, bridging traditional practices with innovative expressions. This synthesis is vital for the contemporary Church, which must navigate the tension between maintaining historical integrity and embracing present realities.

Modern revelation also brings practical changes to worship structures. The traditional liturgical calendar, for example, may now incorporate elements that reflect ongoing divine revelations. Celebrations like Pentecost gain revived significance, resonating with greater intensity as they highlight the ever-present work of the Holy Spirit in the modern world.

Furthermore, modern revelation impacts how worship spaces are designed. There's a growing tendency to craft environments that are not just functional but also profoundly symbolic. Architecture, art, and even the layout of worship areas are influenced by a deeper theological understanding, embodying the presence of God in innovative ways. This aligns with Rahner's view that every aspect of life, including our physical surroundings, can bear the mark of divine grace.

The role of scripture and other sacred texts in devotion also evolves with new revelations. Exegesis now goes beyond historical-critical methods to include contemporary existential and spiritual insights. This causes a richer, more nuanced engagement with the Word of God, enhancing both personal and communal devotion. As written, "The entrance of thy words giveth light; it giveth understanding unto the simple" (Ps. 119:130).

Lastly, modern revelation affects the emotional and psychological dimensions of devotion. By offering new ways of understanding suffering, joy, and the human condition, it shapes a more resilient and adaptive faith. It provides comfort in times of trial and a deeper sense of purpose and calling, urging believers to continually seek God's presence in every circumstance.

To conclude, the impact of modern revelation on worship and devotion is profound and multifaceted. From personal encounters with God to communal expressions of faith, it reshapes every aspect of our spiritual life. It invites us into deeper intimacy, broader communal engagement, and richer expressions of the divine mystery. Thus, modern revelation serves as a continuous call to 'worship the Lord in the beauty of holiness' (Ps. 29:2), enriching our devotion and aligning our lives ever more closely with the divine will.

Contemporary Evangelization Strategies

The ecclesial mission to evangelize has never been more pressing, tasked as it is with bridging the ancient with the modern, the sacred with the secular. In our age of fast-moving technology and pervasive skepticism, the strategies employed must reflect the deep truths of revelation while engaging the curious minds shaped by contemporary experiences.

The first step in crafting effective evangelization strategies lies in understanding the audience. Today, the audience is a paradox: simultaneously more globalized yet increasingly compartmentalized, deeply connected but often spiritually fragmented. This duality demands a multifaceted approach, drawing from the wisdom of our theological forebears while utilizing modern means of communication. "Ye are the light of the world. A city that is set on a hill cannot be hid" (Matt. 5:14). This biblical mandate underscores the visibility and clarity our message must hold, regardless of the medium.

To begin with, digital evangelization cannot be overlooked. Engaging with platforms such as social media, blogs, podcasts, and video channels offers an unprecedented reach. Yet, this is not merely about broadcasting traditional content through new mediums. The message must be adaptable, captivating, and profoundly rooted in theological truths. Gregarious platforms that encourage dialogue, such as forums and comment sections, serve as virtual agora where believers and seekers alike can engage in meaningful discussions. "So then faith cometh by hearing, and hearing by the word of God" (Rom. 10:17). Our mission requires a strong online presence, packed with resources that draw the viewer into deeper inquiry and reflection.

Furthermore, the role of personal testimony has taken on renewed significance. In an age suspicious of institutional authority yet starved for authenticity, personal stories of faith resonate powerfully. These testimonies need to be shared within the local community and globally. The transformative power of an individual's conversion story can often illuminate the most profound theological truths. When woven with scriptural reflections and theological insights, they render abstract concepts tangible. "And they overcame him by the blood of the Lamb, and by the word of their testimony" (Rev. 12:11). This strategy mirrors the narrative style of the Gospels, grounding immense spiritual truths in the lived experiences of individuals.

Additionally, contemporary evangelization should not shy away from intellectual engagement. This involves staging debates, lectures, and seminars that delve into theological, philosophical, and scientific perspectives—a practice harking back to the scholastic tradition of the Church. Karl Rahner's existential philosophy and von Balthasar's dramatic exploration of revelation can serve as fertile grounds for such intellectually stimulating sessions. Forums where science meets faith can dissolve misconceptions that faith is antithetical to reason, reinforcing the unity of truth. "The fear of the Lord is the beginning of knowledge: but fools despise wisdom and instruction" (Prov. 1:7). Engaging the mind fortifies the spirit, building a cohesive framework for understanding revelation.

Community building remains a cornerstone of evangelization. Small faith-sharing groups and ecclesial movements can provide the intimacy and support that larger church gatherings sometimes lack. Here, the teachings of Augustine on the Trinity could be explored deeply, reflecting on the relational nature of God and humanity. By fostering close-knit communities, the Church effectively mirrors the communal life of the early Christians, offering a palpable sense of belonging and purpose. Forging strong social bonds through these groups nurtures a personal relationship with God, echoing the Trinitarian fellowship. "For where two or three are gathered together in my name, there am I in the midst of them" (Matt. 18:20).

Moreover, visual and performing arts offer unique avenues for evangelization. The visceral power of art to convey complex theological truths should be harnessed more deliberately.

Artistic expressions—whether through Byzantine icons reflecting Gregory's Trinitarian insights or contemporary works inspired by Balthasar's aesthetics—serve as windows to the divine, touching parts of the soul that arguments and expositions often cannot. Performances, including plays and liturgical dance, can enact the dramatic narrative of salvation history, providing experiential understanding. "Let everything that hath breath praise the Lord. Praise ye the Lord" (Ps. 150:6). The arts elevate worship and evangelization to a transcendental experience.

Pastoral care, in its most compassionate form, also emerges as a powerful evangelization tool. Ministers and lay leaders, by embodying the love of Christ in actions, provide living testimony to the world. Outreach programs that address social injustices, support the needy, and promote holistic well-being resonate deeply with contemporary audiences seeking tangible evidence of faith in action. The compassionate outreach mirrors Christ's ministry and verifies the Church's commitment to both spiritual and corporal works of mercy. "For I was an hungered, and ye gave me meat: I was thirsty, and ye gave me drink: I was a stranger, and ye took me in" (Matt. 25:35).

Incorporating modern technology, authentic personal testimony, intellectual and artistic engagement, community building, and compassionate outreach forms an intricate tapestry for modern evangelization. This mosaic approach is not just about adherence to tradition but about dynamic engagement with the present world.

Lastly, maintaining an ecumenical spirit invites participation from a broader Christian audience. Collaborations with other Christian denominations demonstrate unity in diversity, reflecting the universality of the Church. Dialogue and partnership with other religious traditions also offer avenues for mutual enrichment and deeper understanding. This inclusiveness is essential in a pluralistic society, where the Church's mission extends beyond its own boundaries. "And other sheep I have, which are not of this fold: them also I must bring, and they shall hear my voice; and there shall be one fold, and one shepherd" (John 10:16).

The strategies for contemporary evangelization must evolve continuously, integrating the wisdom of the past with the demands of the present, always aiming to illuminate the profound mystery of God's revelation in ways that are accessible, engaging, and transformative. Through thoughtful action and divine guidance, we become effective stewards of the Gospel, ensuring its resonance in every heart and every era.

Conclusion

As we stand on the precipice of understanding, gazing both backward into the annals of theological history and forward into the promise of divine revelation, we must consider the intricate tapestries woven by Augustine, Gregory, Rahner, von Balthasar, and Guerra. Each thinker contributed greatly to our comprehension of God's continual communication with humanity, each adding layers of depth and perception to the contemporary Christian experience.

Human understanding of divine revelation is a dynamic and evolving process. Augustine taught us that God is both intimately known and ineffably mysterious. In his contemplation of the Trinity, Augustine brought forth a vision that encompasses love, relationship, and unity. His insights provide a foundational structure for grasping how divine truths might be communicated across the vast chasms of time and cultural change. Augustine's meditations prompt us to remember that God is not a static deity confined to the pages of ancient texts but an active presence seeking communion with us ("In the beginning was the Word..." John 1:1).

Similarly, St. Gregory of Nazianzus's reflections on the Trinity and the procession of the Holy Spirit offer us profound spiritual and intellectual clarity. Gregory's poetic and mystical approach captures the ineffable qualities of God's nature, emphasizing that revelation is not just about knowledge but also about participation. Gregory invites us to enter into the divine mystery experientially, ensuring that we recognize revelation as a lived and living reality.

Karl Rahner's existential and transcendental exploration of revelation urges us to see God's omnipresence in the mundane and the extraordinary. In a world governed by scientific and rational thought, Rahner challenges us to break free from reductive materialism and embrace the mystery that transcends human cognition. His concept of the "anonymous Christian" posits that God's grace operates beyond the visible boundaries of the Church, reminding us that divine revelation is universally accessible ("For where two or three are gathered together in my name, there am I in the midst of them." Matt. 18:20).

In contrast, Hans Urs von Balthasar's dramatic theology presents revelation as an unfolding narrative, a divine drama in which humanity is an active participant. Von Balthasar emphasizes the aesthetic dimension of revelation, portraying divine truth as beautiful and transformative. This approach helps us understand that revelation is not only an intellectual assent to doctrines but also an encounter with beauty and goodness that shapes and changes us at the deepest levels of our being. Through this lens, the cross and resurrection are seen not just as historical events but as the ultimate theophany where God's love is definitively revealed ("God is love." 1 John 4:8).

Elena Guerra, with her focus on the Holy Spirit and Pentecost, brings a charismatic and pneumatological dimension to our understanding of revelation. Her teachings highlight the ongoing activity of the Spirit in renewing the Church and the world. Guerra's emphasis on prayer, discernment, and spiritual gifts calls us to be attentive to the movements of the Spirit in our lives today ("But the Comforter, which is the Holy Ghost... shall teach you all things." John 14:26).

In synthesizing the views of these theological giants, we see that modern revelation cannot be confined to one perspective. Rather, it is a mosaic of insights that reflects the multidimensional nature of God's communication with humanity. The integration of historical and modern perspectives helps us appreciate the continuity and ever-present novelty of divine revelation. This synthesis invites us to live out a faith enriched by the wisdom of the past and attuned to the nuances of the present.

Moreover, revelation in the context of faith and reason demonstrates that true understanding requires both theological insight and philosophical rigor. The dialogue between faith and reason enriches our comprehension of God, ensuring that our belief is both heartfelt and intellectually robust. This dialogue also engages scientific perspectives, reminding us that the quest for truth encompasses all realms of knowledge ("For we know in part, and we prophesy in part." 1 Cor. 13:9).

Practically, understanding modern revelation impacts how we worship and evangelize. It calls us to deepen our personal and communal prayer life, to be open to the transformative power of the Holy Spirit, and to articulate our faith in ways that resonate with contemporary society. Our evangelization strategies must reflect the dynamic and relational nature of God's revelation, focusing on authentic encounters and lived testimonies.

In conclusion, modern revelation—through the combined wisdom of Augustine, Gregory, Rahner, von Balthasar, and Guerra—challenges us to embrace a faith that is both ancient and fresh, both rooted and reaching. This revelation invites us to a deeper relationship with God, calling us to recognize the divine presence in every aspect of our lives and to respond with love, understanding, and action. Thus, our journey toward understanding God is not one of isolation but of collective exploration, where the insights of great theologians guide us in our ongoing pursuit of divine truth.

Appendix A: Appendix

The pursuit of divine wisdom is a journey marked by the intertwining of faith and reason, and our understanding of God's revelation is a testament to this profound synergy. As we delve into the intricacies of theological thought, it becomes apparent that each insight, each revelation, serves as a beacon guiding us closer to the divine truth.

Throughout this work, the theological contributions of Augustine, Gregory, Rahner, von Balthasar, and Guerra have illuminated our path. Their elucidations have provided us with a multifaceted perspective on how God reveals Himself to humanity. These revelations are not static; they evolve as humanity grows in wisdom and understanding, mirroring the journey of faith itself.

In the beginning, Augustine's penetrating insights into the Trinity offered a foundation upon which much of Western Christian theology is built. His reflections on the nature of God as a community of love have profound implications for how we understand divine revelation. As stated in the Scriptures, "God is love" (1 John 4:8), and Augustine's theology echoes this timeless truth.

The journey continued with Gregory of Nazianzus, whose eloquent articulations on the Trinity further enriched our comprehension. His delineation of the distinct yet united persons of the Trinity underscored the mystery of God's revelation, a mystery that invites us to ponder deeply. "For now we see through a glass, darkly; but then face to face" (1 Cor. 13:12), reflecting the ever-deepening revelation of the divine.

Moving forward to the modern era, Karl Rahner's existential approach to theology brought a fresh perspective to divine revelation. His assertion that the human experience is a locus of divine encounter opened new vistas for understanding God's continual self-disclosure. Rahner's thought reminds us that "the kingdom of God is within you" (Luke 17:21), inviting us to recognize the divine in the everyday.

Hans Urs von Balthasar's theodramatic approach added yet another layer to our understanding. His emphasis on the interplay between divine revelation and human response highlights the dynamic nature of our relationship with God. Balthasar's work is a testament to the fact that revelation is not merely received; it is also lived and enacted. "Ye shall know them by their fruits" (Matt. 7:16), a recognition that revelation bears tangible outcomes in the lives of believers.

Blessed Elena Guerra's focus on the Holy Spirit and Pentecost brings the discussion of revelation into a more charismatic and experiential realm. Her teachings remind us of the transformative power of the Spirit, as manifest during Pentecost when "they were all filled with the Holy Ghost, and began to speak with other tongues, as the Spirit gave them utterance" (Acts 2:4). Guerra's insights underscore the ongoing and dynamic nature of divine revelation through the Spirit.

This appendix serves as a recapitulatory reflection on the rich tapestry of theological insights explored in this book. The intersections of thought from Augustine, Gregory, Rahner, von Balthasar, and Guerra reveal a unified yet diverse understanding of how God's revelation continues to unfold in the modern world. Together, they offer a robust framework for engaging with the divine, inviting us to contemplate, to understand, and to live out the truths that have been unveiled.

As we continue to navigate the complexities of faith and reason, let us remain open to the multifaceted revelations of God. For it is through this openness that we come to grasp, albeit imperfectly, the boundless depths of divine wisdom and love.

"The fear of the Lord is the beginning of wisdom" (Prov. 9:10), and it is this reverent pursuit of understanding that we are called to embrace, now and always.

Glossary of Key Terms

This glossary serves as a compendium of pivotal terms essential for grasping the complex and rich tapestry of modern revelation as articulated through the teachings of Augustine, Gregory, Rahner, von Balthasar, and Guerra.

- **Analogia Entis:**

A theological concept describing the analogy of being, which posits that there are resemblances between the Creator (God) and his creations, rooted in the fact that beings created by God can reflect divine qualities. This term is essential in understanding the contexts where comprehension of God stems from observing His creation.

- **Augustinian Trinitarianism:**

This term refers to the model of the Trinity proposed by St. Augustine. It emphasizes the unity of God while recognizing the distinct personhoods within the Godhead. Augustine's insights into the relational aspects of Father, Son, and Holy Spirit continue to influence contemporary theological thought.

- **Biblical Hermeneutics:**

The discipline focused on the interpretation of biblical texts. In the context of modern revelation, it includes understanding how ancient scriptures inform current beliefs and practices. "All scripture is given by inspiration of God, and is profitable for doctrine, for reproof, for correction, for instruction in righteousness" (2 Tim. 3:16).

- **Divine Revelation:**

The act through which God discloses his nature, will, and purpose to humanity, often through scriptures, experiences, and teachings of prophets and saints. It is foundational to the Christian faith and continues to unfold in modern contexts.

- **Ecclesiology:**

The theological study of the Christian Church, its structures, and functions. Understanding the church's role in disseminating and interpreting divine revelation is crucial for integrating historical and modern perspectives.

- **Fundamental Option:**

A concept from Karl Rahner's theology, describing a person's fundamental orientation towards or away from God, which underpins all moral decisions and actions. This orientation is seen as defining one's ultimate relationship with the divine.

- **Kenosis:**

A Greek term meaning 'self-emptying,' used to describe Jesus Christ's renunciation of his divine privileges in the incarnation. It is a central theme in understanding the humility and sacrifice involved in divine revelation.

- **Logos:**

A term meaning 'word' or 'reason,' crucial in Christian theology for describing Jesus Christ as the incarnate Word of God. "In the beginning was the Word, and the Word was with God, and the Word was God" (John 1:1).

- **Modernism:**

A movement characterized by a critical approach to traditional doctrine and practices, questioning established interpretations and emphasizing the relevance of revelation in the modern world.

- **Ontological Difference:**

The distinction between being itself (God) and the beings created by God. This concept is key to understanding different theological perspectives, especially those of Augustine and Gregory, on the transcendence and immanence of God.

- **Perichoresis:**

A theological term used to describe the mutual indwelling and interpenetration of the three persons of the Trinity, without loss of individual identity. This concept is central to understanding the relational ontology of God.

- **Pneumatology:**

The study of the Holy Spirit's nature and works. Blessed Elena Guerra's focus on Pentecost and the Spirit's ongoing activity in the Church exemplifies contemporary engagement with this field.

- **Sacred Tradition:**

The living transmission of the message of the Gospel in the Church. Distinct from scripture but complementary to it, tradition is integral to understanding the full scope of divine revelation.

- **Spirit of Vatican II:**

Refers to the perceived progressive, reform-minded ethos that emerged from the Second Vatican Council. It often involves openness to modern insights and integration with traditional beliefs.

- **Theodicy:**

The branch of theology that grapples with the problem of evil in the world, seeking to reconcile it with the goodness and omnipotence of God. It often intersects with discussions on revelation and divine justice.

- **Theophany:**

An appearance or manifestation of God to humans, often considered a pivotal moment of revelation. Biblical examples include the burning bush (Exod. 3:2) and the transfiguration of Jesus (Matt. 17:2).

- **Trinitarian Theology:**

The study of the Trinity, focusing on the relationship and interactions between Father, Son, and Holy Spirit. Critical for understanding the unity and diversity within God as seen through the perspectives of theologians like Augustine and Gregory.

- **Ubiquity:**

The attribute of God's presence everywhere at all times. "Whither shall I go from thy spirit? or whither shall I flee from thy presence?" (Ps. 139:7).

- **Via Negativa:**

Also known as apophatic theology, this approach speaks of God by negation, emphasizing what He is not rather than descriptive affirmations. It contrasts with via positiva, which affirms God's attributes based on analogy.

Selected Bibliography

In constructing this work on the modern revelation of God, it has been imperative to delve deeply into primary and secondary scholarly sources that enhance our understanding of Augustine, Gregory, Rahner, von Balthasar, and Guerra. The selection was guided by a desire to present a comprehensive and nuanced interpretation of these significant theologians and their views on divine revelation. Balancing the historical breadth with the depth of contemporary scholarship, the following bibliography encompasses seminal books, influential articles, and relevant biblical texts that have been pivotal for each chapter's exploration.

Primary Works

- *Confessions* by Saint Augustine – In this autobiographical work, Augustine articulates his conversion experience and foundational theological developments, providing insights into his understanding of God and revelation.

- *City of God* by Saint Augustine – A critical text for understanding Augustine's perception of the divine nature and the unfolding of God's revelation within the historical context of humanity.

- *Orations* by Saint Gregory of Nazianzus – A collection of Gregory's theological and oratorical masterpieces, offering profound reflections on the Trinity and divine mysteries.

- *Foundations of Christian Faith* by Karl Rahner – This work systematizes Rahner's theological thoughts, focusing on the relationship between human experience and divine revelation.

- *The Glory of the Lord* by Hans Urs von Balthasar – Balthasar's magnum opus, presenting his aesthetic and theological vision of God's revelation through beauty.

Secondary Sources

- *The Theology of Karl Rahner* by Karen Kilby – An essential secondary source that critically analyses Rahner's contributions to modern theology and the interpretation of divine revelation.

- *Balthasar: A (Very) Critical Introduction* by Karen Kilby – This insightful text offers a careful critique and appreciation of von Balthasar's theological methodology and its implications for contemporary thought.

- *St. Gregory of Nazianzus: An Intellectual Biography* by John Anthony McGuckin – McGuckin provides a detailed account of Gregory's life, writings, and theological contributions, elucidating his views on the Trinity and revelation.

- *Augustine Through the Ages: An Encyclopedia* edited by Allan D. Fitzgerald – A comprehensive reference work that covers the entirety of Augustine's thought, including his doctrines on the Trinity and divine revelation.

- *Elena Guerra: The Fatima of the Holy Spirit* by Joan Carroll Cruz – This biography examines Guerra's life and her influence on modern Pentecostal spirituality.

The biblical references have been crucial for embedding theological concepts within the sacred context. The King James Version of the Bible has been the translation of choice, providing familiarity and linguistic beauty. Key passages include:

- "In the beginning was the Word, and the Word was with God, and the Word was God." (John 1:1)

- "But the Comforter, which is the Holy Ghost, whom the Father will send in my name, he shall teach you all things, and bring all things to your remembrance, whatsoever I have said unto you." (John 14:26)

- "For there are three that bear record in heaven, the Father, the Word, and the Holy Ghost: and these three are one." (1 John 5:7)

Academic Articles and Journals

- "Rahner's Theory of Anonymous Christians and Its Implications" in Theological Studies Journal – An analysis of Rahner's concept of anonymous Christianity and its broader implications for understanding revelation in the modern world.

- "The Theology of Hans Urs von Balthasar: Magnificence and Mystery" from Communio – Offers an in-depth exploration of von Balthasar's theological landscape, particularly his views on the mystery of God's revelation.

- "Augustine's Trinitarian Doctrine within the Modern Context" in Augustinian Studies – This article situates Augustine's Trinitarian theology within modern theological discourse, examining its enduring relevance.

- "Gregory of Nazianzus and the Renewal of Trinitarian Theology" in The Patristic and Byzantine Review – A study of Gregory's contributions to Trinitarian theology and their contemporary applications.

- "Elena Guerra's Impact on Modern Charismatic Movements" in Pentecost Studies – This article links Guerra's teachings to the modern Pentecostal and Charismatic movements, highlighting her influence on contemporary spirituality.

Theological Dictionaries and Encyclopedias

- *The Oxford Handbook of Systematic Theology* – This reference provides perspectives on key theological concepts related to divine revelation from multiple renowned theologians.

- *The New Westminster Dictionary of Church History* – A critical resource for understanding the historical development of theological thought, particularly in relation to the figures discussed.

- *Dictionary of Christian Biography* by Henry Wace – Offers biographical insights into the lives of influential Christian theologians, including those central to this study.

In addition to these foundational texts, numerous works of critical and interpretive scholarship have been consulted to ensure a robust and thorough treatment of the subject matter. It is this deep reservoir of resources that underpins the discussion of modern divine revelation as interpreted through the lens of the chosen theologians and philosophers.

This selected bibliography is not exhaustive, but it represents the core of the research foundation. It is our hope that these readings will not only support the arguments presented but also serve as a guide for further study and contemplation on the profound mystery of God's revelation in the modern era.

THE 15 PRAYERS OF ST. BRIDGET

These Prayers and these Promises have been copied from a book printed in Toulouse in 1740 and published by the P. Adrien Parvilliers of the Company of Jesus, Apostolic Missionary of the Holy Land, with approbation, permission and recommendation to distribute them.
Pope Pius IX took cognisance of these Prayers with the prologue; he approved them May 31, 1862, recognising them as true and for the good of souls.

As St. Bridget for a long time wanted to know the number of blows Our Lord received during His Passion, He one day appeared to her and said: "I received 5480 blows on My Body. If you wish to honour them in some way, say 15 Our Fathers and 15 Hail Marys with the following Prayers (which He taught her) for a whole year. When the year is up, you will have honoured each one of My Wounds."

He made the following promises to anyone who recited these Prayers for a whole year:

1. I will deliver 15 souls of his lineage from Purgatory.
2. 15 souls of his lineage will be confirmed and preserved in grace.
3. 15 sinners of his lineage will be converted.
4. Whoever recites these Prayers will attain the first degree of perfection.
5. 15 days before his death I will give him My Precious Body in order that he may escape eternal starvation; I will give him My Precious Blood to drink lest he thirst eternally.
6. 15 days before his death he will feel a deep contrition for all his sins and will have a perfect knowledge of them.
7. I will place before him the sign of My Victorious Cross for his help and defence against the attacks of his enemies.

8. Before his death I shall come with My Dearest Beloved Mother.

9. I shall graciously receive his soul, and will lead it into eternal joys.

10. And having led it there I shall give him a special draught from the fountain of My Deity, something I will not for those who have not recited My Prayers.

11. Let it be known that whoever may have been living in a state of mortal sin for 30 years, but who will recite devoutly, or have the intention to recite these Prayers, the Lord will forgive him all his sins.

12. I shall protect him from strong temptations.

13. I shall preserve and guard his 5 senses.

14. I shall preserve him from a sudden death.

15. His soul will be delivered from eternal death.

16. He will obtain all he asks for from God and the Blessed Virgin.

17. If he has lived all his life doing his own will and he is to die the next day, his life will be prolonged.

18. Every time one recites these Prayers he gains 100 days indulgence.

19. He is assured of being joined to the supreme Choir of Angels.

20. Whoever teaches these Prayers to another, will have continuous joy and merit which will endure eternally.

21. There where these Prayers are being said or will be said in the future God is present with His grace.

Each prayer is preceded by one Our Father and one Hail Mary.

Our Father, who art in heaven, hallowed be thy name.
Thy kingdom come.
Thy will be done on earth as it is in heaven.
Give us this day our daily bread and forgive us our

trespasses as we forgive those who trespass against us and lead us not into temptation but deliver us from evil. **Amen**

Hail Mary, full of grace, the Lord is with thee; blessed art thou among women and blessed is the fruit of thy womb, Jesus.
Holy Mary, Mother of God, pray for us sinners, now and at the hour of our death. **Amen.**

FIRST PRAYER
Our Father – Hail Mary.
O Jesus Christ! Eternal Sweetness to those who love Thee, joy surpassing all joy and all desire, Salvation and Hope of all sinners, Who hast proved that Thou hast no greater desire than to be among men, even assuming human nature at the fullness of time for the love of men, recall all the sufferings Thou hast endured from the instant of Thy conception, and especially during Thy Passion, as it was decreed and ordained from all eternity in the Divine plan.

Remember, O Lord, that during the Last Supper with Thy disciples, having washed their feet, Thou gavest them Thy Most Precious Body and Blood, and while at the same time thou didst sweetly console them, Thou didst foretell them Thy coming Passion.
Remember the sadness and bitterness which Thou didst experience in Thy Soul as Thou Thyself bore witness saying: "My Soul is sorrowful even unto death."

Remember all the fear, anguish and pain that Thou didst suffer in Thy delicate Body before the torment of the Crucifixion, when, after having prayed three times, bathed in a sweat of blood, Thou wast betrayed by Judas, Thy disciple, arrested by the people of a nation Thou hadst chosen and elevated, accused by false witnesses, unjustly judged by three judges during the flower of Thy youth and during the solemn Paschal season.

Remember that Thou wast despoiled of Thy garments and clothed in those of derision; that Thy Face and Eyes were veiled, that Thou wast buffeted, crowned with thorns, a reed placed in Thy Hands, that Thou was crushed with blows and overwhelmed with affronts and outrages.
In memory of all these pains and sufferings which Thou didst endure before Thy Passion on the Cross, grant me before my death true contrition, a sincere and entire confession, worthy satisfaction and the remission of all my sins. **Amen.**

SECOND PRAYER
Our Father – Hail Mary.
O Jesus! True liberty of angels, Paradise of delights, remember the horror and sadness which Thou didst endure when Thy enemies, like furious lions, surrounded Thee, and by thousands of insults, spits, blows, lacerations and other unheard-of-cruelties, tormented Thee at will.

In consideration of these torments and insulting words, I beseech Thee, O my Saviour, to deliver me from all my enemies, visible and invisible, and to bring me, under Thy protection, to the perfection of eternal salvation. **Amen.**

THIRD PRAYER
Our Father – Hail Mary.
O Jesus! Creator of Heaven and earth Whom nothing can encompass or limit, Thou Who dost enfold and hold all under Thy Loving power, remember the very bitter pain.

Thou didst suffer when the Jews nailed Thy Sacred Hands and Feet to the Cross by blow after blow with big blunt nails, and not finding Thee in a pitiable enough state to satisfy their rage, they enlarged Thy Wounds, and added pain to pain, and with indescribable cruelty stretched Thy Body on the Cross, pulled Thee from all sides, thus dislocating Thy Limbs.

I beg of Thee, O Jesus, by the memory of this most Loving suffering of the Cross, to grant me the grace to fear Thee and to Love Thee. **Amen.**

FOURTH PRAYER
Our Father - Hail Mary.
O Jesus! Heavenly Physician, raised aloft on the Cross to heal our wounds with Thine, remember the bruises which Thou didst suffer and the weakness of all Thy Members which were distended to such a degree that never was there pain like unto Thine.

From the crown of Thy Head to the Soles of Thy Feet there was not one spot on Thy Body that was not in torment, and yet, forgetting all Thy sufferings, Thou didst not cease to pray to Thy Heavenly Father for Thy enemies, saying: "Father forgive them for they know not what they do."

Through this great Mercy, and in memory of this suffering, grant that the remembrance of Thy Most Bitter Passion may effect in us a perfect contrition and the remission of all our sins. **Amen**.

FIFTH PRAYER
Our Father - Hail Mary.
O Jesus! Mirror of eternal splendour, remember the sadness which Thou experienced, when contemplating in the light of Thy Divinity the predestination of those who would be saved by the merits of Thy Sacred Passion.

Thou didst see at the same time, the great multitude of reprobates who would be damned for their sins, and Thou didst complain bitterly of those hopeless lost and unfortunate sinners.

Through this abyss of compassion and pity, and especially through the goodness which Thou displayed to the good thief when Thou saidst to him: "This day, thou shalt be with Me in Paradise." I beg of Thee, O Sweet Jesus, that at the hour of my death, Thou wilt show me mercy. **Amen**.

SIXTH PRAYER
Our Father - Hail Mary.
O Jesus! Beloved and most desirable King, remember the grief Thou didst suffer, when naked and like a common criminal.

Thou was fastened and raised on the Cross, when all Thy relatives and friends abandoned Thee, except Thy Beloved Mother, who remained close to Thee during Thy agony and whom Thou didst entrust to Thy faithful disciple when Thou saidst to Mary: "Woman, behold thy son!" and to St. John: "Son, behold thy Mother!"

I beg of Thee O my Saviour, by the sword of sorrow which pierced the soul of Thy holy Mother, to have compassion on me in all my affliction and tribulations, both corporal and spiritual, and to assist me in all my trials, and especially at the hour of my death. **Amen**.

SEVENTH PRAYER
Our Father - Hail Mary.
O Jesus! Inexhaustible Fountain of compassion, Who by a profound gesture of Love, said from the Cross: "I thirst!" suffered from the thirst for the salvation of the human race.

I beg of Thee O my Saviour, to inflame in our hearts the desire to tend toward perfection in all our acts; and to extinguish in us the concupiscence of the flesh and the ardor of worldly desires. **Amen**.

EIGHTH PRAYER
Our Father – Hail Mary.
O Jesus! Sweetness of hearts, delight of the spirit, by the bitterness of the vinegar and gall which Thou didst taste on the Cross for Love of us, grant us the grace to receive worthily.

Thy Precious Body and Blood during our life and at the hour of our death, that they may serve as a remedy and consolation for our souls. **Amen.**

NINTH PRAYER
Our Father – Hail Mary.
O Jesus! Royal virtue, joy of the mind, recall the pain Thou didst endure when, plunged in an ocean of bitterness at the approach of death, insulted, outraged by the Jews.

Thou didst cry out in a loud voice that Thou was abandoned by Thy Father, saying: "My God, My God, why hast Thou forsaken me?"

Through this anguish, I beg of Thee, O my Saviour, not to abandon me in the terrors and pains of my death. **Amen.**

TENTH PRAYER
Our Father – Hail Mary.
O Jesus! Who art the beginning and end of all things, life and virtue, remembers that for our sakes Thou was plunged in an abyss of suffering from the soles of Thy Feet to the crown of Thy Head.

In consideration of the enormity of Thy Wounds, teach me to keep, through pure love, Thy Commandments, whose way is wide and easy for those who love Thee. **Amen.**

ELEVENTH PRAYER
Our Father - Hail Mary.
O Jesus! Deep abyss of mercy, I beg of Thee, in memory of Thy Wounds which penetrated to the very marrow of Thy Bones and to the depth of Thy being, to draw me, a miserable sinner, overwhelmed by my offenses, away from sin and to hide me from Thy Face justly irritated against me, hide me in Thy wounds, until Thy anger and just indignation shall have passed away. **Amen.**

TWELFTH PRAYER
Our Father - Hail Mary.
O Jesus! Mirror of Truth, symbol of unity, bond of charity, remember the multitude of wounds with which Thou wast afflicted from head to foot, torn and reddened by the spilling of Thy adorable Blood. O great and universal pain, which Thou didst suffer in Thy virginal flesh for love of us! Sweetest Jesus! What is there that Thou couldst have done for us which Thou has not done!

May the fruit of Thy suffering be renewed in my soul by the faithful remembrance of Thy Passion, and may Thy love increase in my heart each day, until I see Thee in eternity: Thou Who art the treasure of every real good and every joy, which I beg Thee to grant me, O Sweetest Jesus, in heaven. **Amen.**

THIRTEENTH PRAYER
Our Father - Hail Mary.
O Jesus! Strong Lion, Immortal and Invincible King, remember the pain which Thou didst endure when all Thy strength, both moral and physical, was entirely exhausted, Thou didst bow Thy Head, saying: "It is consummated!"

Through this anguish and grief, I beg of Thee Lord Jesus, to

have mercy on me at the hour of my death when my mind
will be greatly troubled and my soul will be in
anguish. **Amen.**

FOURTEENTH PRAYER
Our Father - Hail Mary.
O Jesus! Only Son of the Father, Splendour and Figure of His
Substance, remember the simple and humble
recommendation.

Thou didst make of Thy Soul to Thy Eternal Father, saying:
"Father, into Thy Hands I commend My Spirit!" And with Thy
Body all torn, and Thy Heart Broken, and the bowels of
Thy Mercy open to redeem us, Thou didst Expire.

By this Precious Death, I beg of Thee O King of Saints,
comfort me and help me to resist the devil, the flesh and the
world, so that being dead to the world I may live for Thee
alone.

I beg of Thee at the hour of my death to receive me, a
pilgrim and an exile returning to Thee. **Amen.**

FIFTEENTH PRAYER
Our Father - Hail Mary.
O Jesus! True and fruitful Vine! Remember the abundant
outpouring of Blood which Thou didst so generously shed
from Thy Sacred Body as juice from grapes in a wine press.

From Thy Side, pierced with a lance by a soldier, blood and
water issued forth until there was not left in Thy Body a
single drop, and finally, like a bundle of myrrh lifted to the
top of the Cross Thy delicate Flesh was destroyed, the very
Substance of Thy Body withered, and the Marrow of Thy
Bones dried up.

Through this bitter Passion and through the outpouring of Thy Precious Blood, I beg of Thee, O Sweet Jesus, to receive my soul when I am in my death agony. **Amen.**

CONCLUSION
O Sweet Jesus! Pierce my heart so that my tears of penitence and love will be my bread day and night; may I be converted entirely to Thee, may my heart be Thy perpetual habitation, may my conversation be pleasing to Thee, and may the end of my life be so praiseworthy that I may merit Heaven and there with Thy saints, praise Thee forever. **Amen.**